Especially for

....

From

....

Date

....

The
BIBLE
PROMISE
BOOK®
for Women

Prayer Edition

BARBOUR
PUBLISHING

Chapter introductions written by Tina Krause.

Prayers are taken from *Prayers from the Heart,* published by Barbour Publishing, Inc. All rights reserved.

ISBN 978-1-64352-935-6

Published by Barbour Publishing, Inc., 1810 Barbour Drive, Uhrichsville, Ohio 44683, www.barbourbooks.com

Our mission is to inspire the world with the life-changing message of the Bible.

 Member of the
Evangelical Christian
Publishers Association

Printed in China.

Contents

Introduction

Our world sends many conflicting signals on the important issues of life. How should we approach anger? Is discipline a good thing or not? Why speak with honesty? Is prayer for real? What is true wisdom?

In His kindness, God has answered all of these questions—and many more—in the pages of His Word, the Bible. Whatever our needs, we can find in scripture the principles we need to address the issues we face.

This collection of Bible verses is a handy reference to some of the key issues that all people—and especially women—face. In these pages, you'll find carefully selected verses that address topics like comfort, encouragement, friendship, purity, rest, and understanding. In fact, more than five dozen categories are covered, arranged alphabetically for ease of use.

This book is not intended to replace regular, personal Bible study. Nor is it a replacement for a good concordance for in-depth study of a particular subject. It is, however, a quick reference to some of the key issues of life that women most often face. We hope it will be an encouragement to you as you read.

Adversity

*N*o one is exempt from problems. From the palace to the poorhouse, women throughout the ages have fought and conquered adversity in their lives.

Queen Esther risked losing her only relative and her people. Using her influence, she saved the Israelites from destruction. Interestingly, the Jewish name *Esther* means "Hadassah," which comes from the word *myrtle*—the tree whose leaves only release fragrance when they are crushed.

Are you facing adversity? Perhaps your faith has brought reproach, or daily struggles have robbed your faith. Regardless, the scriptures ease the crush of adversity, releasing the sweet fragrance of God's overcoming power.

Lord, I know I can't hope to escape every
unpleasant circumstance in this world. Just the same,
I will trust in You, whatever comes. Protect me in the
way You see fit, in the way that best advances
Your purpose for my life. Amen.

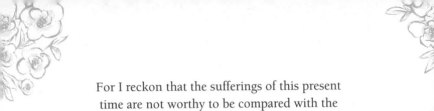

For I reckon that the sufferings of this present
time are not worthy to be compared with the
glory which shall be revealed in us.
ROMANS 8:18 KJV

For just as we share abundantly in the sufferings of Christ,
so also our comfort abounds through Christ. If we are distressed,
it is for your comfort and salvation; if we are comforted,
it is for your comfort, which produces in you
patient endurance of the same sufferings we suffer.
2 CORINTHIANS 1:5–6 NIV

If you are reviled for the name of Christ, you are blessed,
because the Spirit of glory and of God rests on you.
1 PETER 4:14 NASB

"These things I have spoken to you, that in Me you
may have peace. In the world you will have tribulation;
but be of good cheer, I have overcome the world."
JOHN 16:33 NKJV

In the midst of suffering, I want to keep my eyes on You, Jesus.
The suffering You endured for my sake makes my trials look
like nothing. Help me look forward to the promise and to
forget the temporary troubles I have now. Amen.

That the trial of your faith, being much more precious than of gold
that perisheth, though it be tried with fire, might be found unto
praise and honour and glory at the appearing of Jesus Christ.
1 PETER 1:7 KJV

Are any of you suffering hardships?
You should pray.
JAMES 5:13 NLT

I want to know Christ and experience the mighty power
that raised him from the dead. I want to suffer with him,
sharing in his death, so that one way or another I will
experience the resurrection from the dead!
PHILIPPIANS 3:10–11 NLT

After you have suffered for a little while, the God of all grace,
who called you to His eternal glory in Christ, will Himself
perfect, confirm, strengthen and establish you.
1 PETER 5:10 NASB

"Blessed are you when men hate you, and when
they exclude you, and revile you, and cast out
your name as evil, for the Son of Man's sake."
LUKE 6:22 NKJV

Yea, and all that will live godly in Christ Jesus
shall suffer persecution.
2 TIMOTHY 3:12 KJV

Lord, I know bad things will come my way in life,
but I am secure in Your love that never fails. I am constantly
blessed by Your care and concern. I am so important to You
that even the hairs of my head are all numbered. Amen.

For momentary, light affliction is producing for us
an eternal weight of glory far beyond all comparison.
2 CORINTHIANS 4:17 NASB

Dear friends, do not be surprised at the fiery ordeal
that has come on you to test you, as though something
strange were happening to you. But rejoice inasmuch
as you participate in the sufferings of Christ, so that
you may be overjoyed when his glory is revealed.
1 PETER 4:12–13 NIV

If we suffer, we shall also reign with him.
2 TIMOTHY 2:12 KJV

For this is commendable, if because of conscience toward God
one endures grief, suffering wrongfully. . . . For to this you were
called, because Christ also suffered for us, leaving us an example,
that you should follow His steps: "Who committed no sin,
nor was deceit found in His mouth"; who, when He was reviled,
did not revile in return; when He suffered, He did not threaten,
but committed Himself to Him who judges righteously.
1 PETER 2:19, 21–23 NKJV

*Our Creator never intended that we should
shoulder a load of suffering ourselves.
That's the whole purpose of spiritual community.*
LINDA BARTLETT

Angels

A near miss. Your car swerves to the side of the road avoiding a collision with an oncoming vehicle. How did you avoid disaster? Fatigue zaps your strength but you still have much to do. You pray and amazingly you breeze through your work as if unseen hands carried you to complete the task. A coincidence? Or did God dispatch angels to assist you?

Angels are real. Unlike the stereotypical images of chubby-cheeked cherubs, these powerful, angelic beings minister to believers. At God's command, they delivered Paul from prison, shut the lions' mouths, provided for Elijah, and brought an amazing message to Mary.

Chubby-cheeked cherubs? Think again.

Heavenly Father, the world is a frightening place.
I look around and see endless opportunities for disaster
and tragedy. And yet, I place my trust in Your promise
to send Your angels to watch over and guard me.
Thank You for Your protection. Amen.

And God never said to any of the angels, "Sit in the place of honor
at my right hand until I humble your enemies, making them
a footstool under your feet." Therefore, angels are only servants—
spirits sent to care for people who will inherit salvation.
HEBREWS 1:13–14 NLT

And he shall send his angels with a great sound
of a trumpet, and they shall gather together his elect from
the four winds, from one end of heaven to the other.
MATTHEW 24:31 KJV

The angel of the LORD encamps around
those who fear Him, and rescues them.
PSALM 34:7 NASB

For I am persuaded that neither death nor life,
nor angels nor principalities nor powers,
nor things present nor things to come,
nor height nor depth, nor any other created thing,
shall be able to separate us from the love of
God which is in Christ Jesus our Lord.
ROMANS 8:38–39 NKJV

On life's busy thoroughfares
We meet with angels unawares.
HELEN STEINER RICE

Anger

*I*t doesn't matter who was right or wrong. You feel wronged and anger simmers on the verge of full boil.

Can we be angry and not sin? To feel anger is one thing, to act on it is another. When we use our anger to justify our wrongful deeds, we sin.

The Bible, however, gives us clear and concise instructions on how to handle anger or angry people. How can we curb anger, irritations, and flare-ups? Apply the calming influence of God's Word to our circumstance. Ah, yes. That's better.

Lord, help me be the peacekeeper, never the one
who stirs up more anger. Help me be an
example to my whole family. Amen.

He who is slow to anger has great understanding,
but he who is quick-tempered exalts folly.
PROVERBS 14:29 NASB

So then, my beloved brethren, let every man be swift to hear,
slow to speak, slow to wrath; for the wrath of man does
not produce the righteousness of God.
JAMES 1:19–20 NKJV

Don't befriend angry people or associate with hot-tempered people,
or you will learn to be like them and endanger your soul.
PROVERBS 22:24–25 NLT

Be not hasty in thy spirit to be angry:
for anger resteth in the bosom of fools.
ECCLESIASTES 7:9 KJV

Better to live in a desert than with a
quarrelsome and nagging wife.
PROVERBS 21:19 NIV

*Today in anger, I said something I shouldn't have. Forgive me, Lord.
Instead of speaking in anger and frustration, I want to fill my
mouth with words of continual praise to You. Amen.*

Fathers, do not exasperate your children,
so that they will not lose heart.
COLOSSIANS 3:21 NASB

A soft answer turns away wrath,
but a harsh word stirs up anger.
PROVERBS 15:1 NKJV

Do everything without complaining and arguing.
PHILIPPIANS 2:14 NLT

But I say, if you are even angry with someone, you are subject
to judgment! If you call someone an idiot, you are in danger
of being brought before the court. And if you curse
someone, you are in danger of the fires of hell.
MATTHEW 5:22 NLT

A wrathful man stirreth up strife:
but he that is slow to anger appeaseth strife.
PROVERBS 15:18 KJV

He who is slow to anger is better than the mighty,
and he who rules his spirit, than he who captures a city.
PROVERBS 16:32 NASB

*Lord, in the heat of anger, control my tongue,
because what I say then can be as damaging to my
soul as it is to my victim's reputation. Amen.*

Beloved, do not avenge yourselves,
but rather give place to wrath;
for it is written, "Vengeance is Mine,
I will repay," says the Lord.
ROMANS 12:19 NKJV

Better a dry crust eaten in peace than
a house filled with feasting—and conflict.
PROVERBS 17:1 NLT

"In your anger do not sin": Do not let the
sun go down while you are still angry.
EPHESIANS 4:26 NIV

*Being angry or unforgiving makes
it impossible to have a gentle and quiet spirit.*
DARLENE WILKINSON

Charity

*W*omen are caregivers by nature. Need a hand? We offer two! Yet sometimes our gift of giving wears old under constant demands and daily responsibilities.

God, however, is the supreme example of charity at work. He saw our neediness and sent His Son, Jesus, to save us from our sins. And He keeps on giving.

Having received so much compels us to give more liberally. God's charity never ceases and neither should ours. Although needs differ—financial, physical, emotional, or spiritual—human benevolence comes from a giving heart. And our charitable giving begins right where we are.

Lord, help me to be charitable in all that I do.
My acts of charity reflect on You, and I want
to bring honor to You at all times. Amen.

Blessed is he that considereth the poor: the Lord will deliver him in time of trouble. The Lord will preserve him, and keep him alive; and he shall be blessed upon the earth: and thou wilt not deliver him unto the will of his enemies.

Psalm 41:1–2 kjv

One who is gracious to a poor man lends to the Lord,
and He will repay him for his good deed.

Proverbs 19:17 nasb

"But when you give a feast, invite the poor, the maimed, the lame, the blind. And you will be blessed, because they cannot repay you; for you shall be repaid at the resurrection of the just."

Luke 14:13–14 nkjv

It is a sin to despise one's neighbor,
but blessed is the one who is kind to the needy.

Proverbs 14:21 niv

I have shewed you all things, how that so labouring ye ought to support the weak, and to remember the words of the Lord Jesus, how he said, It is more blessed to give than to receive.

Acts 20:35 kjv

Father, don't let me feel social pressure when giving. No matter how much or how little I can give, help me to give joyously. Amen.

He has given freely to the poor, His righteousness
endures forever; His horn will be exalted in honor.

Psalm 112:9 nasb

Teach those who are rich in this world not to be proud and not to trust in their money, which is so unreliable. Their trust should be in God, who richly gives us all we need for our enjoyment. Tell them to use their money to do good. They should be rich in good works and generous to those in need, always being ready to share with others. By doing this they will be storing up their treasure as a good foundation for the future so that they may experience true life.

1 TIMOTHY 6:17–19 NLT

Sell that ye have, and give alms; provide yourselves bags which wax not old, a treasure in the heavens that faileth not, where no thief approacheth, neither moth corrupteth. For where your treasure is, there will your heart be also.

LUKE 12:33–34 KJV

Above all, keep fervent in your love for one another, because love covers a multitude of sins. Be hospitable to one another without complaint. As each one has received a special gift, employ it in serving one another as good stewards of the manifold grace of God.

1 PETER 4:8–10 NASB

"Give, and it will be given to you: good measure, pressed down, shaken together, and running over will be put into your bosom. For with the same measure that you use, it will be measured back to you."

LUKE 6:38 NKJV

Charity begins at home.

UNKNOWN

Comfort

A loved one passes away, and friends and family surround you with prayers and comforting words. Illness strikes a blow, but friends support and comfort you. Problems weigh heavy and there seems no way out, but the scriptures speak comfort to your heart.

Moms comfort their sick children with hugs and chicken soup. Similarly, God eases our pain and lightens our load through the comfort of His Word and His Spirit. Jesus called the Holy Spirit "the Comforter." He is the One who teaches, guides, soothes, and stands with us. The Comforter comforts like no one else can.

Lord, remove the fears that bind me so that I can be happy in
the knowledge that You are there to comfort me—
no matter what else is happening. Amen.

Blessed be the God and Father of our Lord Jesus Christ,
the Father of mercies and God of all comfort, who comforts
us in all our tribulation, that we may be able to comfort
those who are in any trouble, with the comfort with
which we ourselves are comforted by God.
2 CORINTHIANS 1:3–4 NKJV

Even when I walk through the darkest valley, I will not
be afraid, for you are close beside me. Your rod
and your staff protect and comfort me.
PSALM 23:4 NLT

" 'He will wipe every tear from their eyes. There will be
no more death or mourning or crying or pain,
for the old order of things has passed away.' "
REVELATION 21:4 NIV

He will swallow up death for all time, and the Lord GOD will wipe
tears away from all faces, and He will remove the reproach of
His people from all the earth; for the LORD has spoken.
ISAIAH 25:8 NASB

*Lord, please increase my inner strength. Remind me that although
I seem powerless, Your power knows no limits and You will provide
whatever strength I need to see me through my current crisis. Amen.*

And I will pray the Father, and he shall give you another
Comforter, that he may abide with you for ever.
JOHN 14:16 KJV

"But as for me, I would seek God,
and I would place my cause before God."
Job 5:8 NASB

You shall increase my greatness,
and comfort me on every side.
Psalm 71:21 NKJV

For the Lord himself shall descend from heaven with a shout,
with the voice of the archangel, and with the trump of God: and the
dead in Christ shall rise first: then we which are alive and remain
shall be caught up together with them in the clouds, to meet
the Lord in the air: and so shall we ever be with the Lord.
Wherefore comfort one another with these words.
1 Thessalonians 4:16–18 KJV

*Lord, life seems overwhelming to me sometimes. Please give me
the abundant wisdom You've promised and help me to relax
in the knowledge that You will guide me. Amen.*

"Teach these new disciples to obey all the commands I have
given you. And be sure of this: I am with you
always, even to the end of the age."
Matthew 28:20 NLT

The Spirit of the Lord GOD is upon me; because the LORD hath
anointed me to preach good tidings unto the meek; he hath sent
me to bind up the brokenhearted, to proclaim liberty to the
captives, and the opening of the prison to them that are bound;
to proclaim the acceptable year of the LORD, and the day
of vengeance of our God; to comfort all that mourn.
ISAIAH 61:1–2 KJV

I will not leave you comfortless: I will come to you.
JOHN 14:18 KJV

Praise be to the God and Father of our Lord Jesus Christ, the Father
of compassion and the God of all comfort, who comforts us in
all our troubles, so that we can comfort those in any trouble
with the comfort we ourselves receive from God. For just
as we share abundantly in the suffering of Christ,
so also our comfort abounds through Christ.
2 CORINTHIANS 1:3–5 NIV

"Come to Me, all who are weary and
heavy-laden, and I will give you rest."
MATTHEW 11:28 NASB

I remembered your judgments of old,
O Lord, and have comforted myself.
Psalm 119:52 nkjv

"I will comfort you there in Jerusalem
as a mother comforts her child."
Isaiah 66:13 nlt

*Father, my trials are not major, so far. But I know that things can
go wrong in an instant. When I cry to You, I know You hear.
Thank You for Your promises and never-ending care. Amen.*

Finally, brethren, farewell. Become complete. Be of good
comfort, be of one mind, live in peace; and the
God of love and peace will be with you.
2 Corinthians 13:11 nkjv

Come near to God and he will come near to you. Wash your hands,
you sinners, and purify your hearts, you double-minded.
James 4:8 niv

*All you really need is the One who promised never to leave or
forsake you—the One who said, "Lo, I am with you always."*
Joni Eareckson Tada

Conversation

*H*ave you ever blurted out the wrong words at the wrong time? Mortified, you wish you could push rewind and start again—but unfortunately, the words are irretrievable.

The scriptures tell us to keep watch over our tongue, and for good reason. Words have the power to create strife or peace, to uplift or destroy, to bless or to curse.

The old adage claims "words will never hurt me." That, however, is untrue. Wrong words *do* hurt, but the right words spoken at the right time have the power to heal and comfort. Words count—so count your words!

O God, help me think before I speak. Put words of kindness
in my mouth that will build up others instead of
destroying them. I desire to be virtuous. Amen.

So also the tongue is a small part of the body, and yet it boasts of great things. See how great a forest is set aflame by such a small fire!
JAMES 3:5 NASB

A word fitly spoken is like apples of gold in settings of silver.
PROVERBS 25:11 NKJV

Don't make rash promises, and don't be hasty in bringing matters before God. After all, God is in heaven, and you are here on earth. So let your words be few.
ECCLESIASTES 5:2 NLT

A gentle answer turns away wrath, but a harsh word stirs up anger.
PROVERBS 15:1 NIV

The heart of the righteous studieth to answer:
but the mouth of the wicked poureth out evil things.
PROVERBS 15:28 KJV

Lord, help my words to be blessings to those
around me in my daily life. Amen.

Let your speech always be with grace, as though seasoned with salt, so that you will know how you should respond to each person.
COLOSSIANS 4:6 NASB

The hearts of the wise make their mouths prudent, and their lips
promote instruction. Gracious words are a honeycomb,
sweet to the soul and healing to the bones.
PROVERBS 16:23–24 NIV

A talebearer revealeth secrets: but he that is of
a faithful spirit concealeth the matter.
PROVERBS 11:13 KJV

He who walks in integrity walks securely, but he
who perverts his ways will be found out.
PROVERBS 10:9 NASB

Even if I should choose to boast, I would not be a fool,
because I would be speaking the truth. But I refrain, so no one
will think more of me than is warranted by what I do or say.
2 CORINTHIANS 12:6 NIV

*Lord, give me self-control over my tongue when vain
or foolish words rise to the surface. Amen.*

A fool vents all his feelings, but a wise man holds them back.
PROVERBS 29:11 NKJV

But now is the time to get rid of anger, rage,
malicious behavior, slander, and dirty language.
COLOSSIANS 3:8 NLT

Set a watch, O Lord, before my mouth; keep the door of my lips.
PSALM 141:3 KJV

There is one who speaks rashly like the thrusts of a sword,
but the tongue of the wise brings healing.
PROVERBS 12:18 NASB

We all stumble in many ways. Anyone who is never at fault in what
they say, is perfect, able to keep their whole body in check.
JAMES 3:2 NIV

*Lord, the next time I am angry, guide me away from sin until I can
speak words of peace and comfort once again. Amen.*

A man has joy by the answer of his mouth, and a word
spoken in due season, how good it is!
PROVERBS 15:23 NKJV

A time to tear and a time to mend.
A time to be quiet and a time to speak.
ECCLESIASTES 3:7 NLT

*Kind words can be short and easy to speak,
but their echoes are truly endless.*
MOTHER TERESA

Counsel

*W*ere you ever so immersed in a problem that you felt like you were drowning? Have you ever had to make a decision and didn't know what to do? At those times we turn to God—often through godly counsel, perhaps from a pastor or trusted Christian friend.

We all need counsel and direction sometimes. The old saying that "two heads are better than one" is not only noteworthy, it's scriptural!

King Solomon said that to seek godly counsel is wise. Moreover, to grow spiritually we must maintain an open, teachable spirit.

Good advice comes from God-advice. Now that's good counsel.

Lord, if there's one thing I need, it's trustworthy guidance. In darkness or light, on fair days or foul, I trust that the light of Your Word will bring me safely home. Amen.

As every man hath received the gift, even so minister the same one to another, as good stewards of the manifold grace of God.
1 PETER 4:10 KJV

For a child will be born to us, a son will be given to us; and the government will rest on His shoulders; and His name will be called Wonderful Counselor, Mighty God, Eternal Father, Prince of Peace.
ISAIAH 9:6 NASB

"All your children will be taught by the LORD,
and great will be their peace."
ISAIAH 54:13 NIV

Now no chastening seems to be joyful for the present,
but painful; nevertheless, afterward it yields the peaceable fruit
of righteousness to those who have been trained by it.
HEBREWS 12:11 NKJV

Get all the advice and instruction you can, so you
will be wise the rest of your life.
PROVERBS 19:20 NLT

*Lord, guard my tongue as I teach my children. Season my speech
with grace—to encourage my children and remind
them to walk in Your path. Amen.*

Howbeit when he, the Spirit of truth, is come, he will guide you into all truth: for he shall not speak of himself; but whatsoever he shall hear, that shall he speak: and he will shew you things to come.
JOHN 16:13 KJV

Where no counsel is, the people fall: but in the
multitude of counsellors there is safety.
PROVERBS 11:14 KJV

Without consultation, plans are frustrated,
but with many counselors they succeed.
PROVERBS 15:22 NASB

"Because the Lord disciplines the one he loves, and he chastens everyone he accepts as his son." Endure hardship as discipline; God is treating you as his children. For what children are not disciplined by their father?
HEBREWS 12:6–7 NIV

A wise man will hear and increase learning, and a man of
understanding will attain wise counsel.
PROVERBS 1:5 NKJV

*Lord, show me my errors and teach me the
proper way to take advice. Amen.*

Two are better than one, because they have a good return for their labor: if either of them falls down, one can help the other up. But pity anyone who falls and has no one to help them up!

ECCLESIASTES 4:9–10 NIV

The true secret of giving advice is, after you have honestly given it, to be perfectly indifferent whether it is taken or not, and never persist in trying to set people right.

HANNAH WHITALL SMITH

Courage

$\mathcal{F}$ew of us require the kind of courage that Daniel had when he entered the lions' den, or that David exercised when he confronted the giant. Nevertheless, courage is needed to conquer our fears, proclaim our faith, and overcome adversity. Oftentimes, we need courage just to get through the day!

The following verses provide instructions and admonitions to build our faith and fortitude. They equip us with the courage we need to conquer our giants in life's den of lions.

Lord, when it comes to courage, I have none of my own. Without You, I would be filled with fear, terrified of a future I cannot see. Thank You for patiently taking my hand and helping me face my fears. Amen.

"Be strong and very courageous. Be careful to obey all the instructions Moses gave you. Do not deviate from them, turning either to the right or to the left. Then you will be successful in everything you do."

Joshua 1:7 NLT

Wait on the Lord: be of good courage, and he shall strengthen thine heart: wait, I say, on the Lord.

Psalm 27:14 KJV

For God has not given us a spirit of timidity, but of power and love and discipline.

2 Timothy 1:7 NASB

So we say with confidence, "The Lord is my helper; I will not be afraid. What can mere mortals do to me?"

Hebrews 13:6 NIV

Only let your conduct be worthy of the gospel of Christ, so that whether I come and see you or am absent, I may hear of your affairs, that you stand fast in one spirit, with one mind striving together for the faith of the gospel, and not in any way terrified by your adversaries, which is to them a proof of perdition, but to you of salvation, and that from God.

Philippians 1:27–28 NKJV

The wicked flee though no one pursues, but the righteous are as bold as a lion.

Proverbs 28:1 NIV

Lord, I've often found myself afraid. Please help me remember where my strength and salvation come from and to say with confidence, "Whom shall I fear? Of whom shall I be afraid?" Amen.

And now, dear children, remain in fellowship with Christ so
that when he returns, you will be full of courage
and not shrink back from him in shame.
1 JOHN 2:28 NLT

Therefore, brethren, having boldness to enter the Holiest by the
blood of Jesus, by a new and living way which He consecrated
for us, through the veil, that is, His flesh, and having a High
Priest over the house of God, let us draw near with
a true heart in full assurance of faith.
HEBREWS 10:19–22 NKJV

So be strong and courageous,
all you who put your hope in the LORD!
PSALM 31:24 NLT

In whom we have boldness and access with
confidence by the faith of him.
EPHESIANS 3:12 KJV

*You have to accept whatever comes and the only important thing is
that you meet it with courage, and with the best you have to give.*
ELEANOR ROOSEVELT

Diligence

*T*he author of Ecclesiastes wrote: "Whatever your hand finds to do, do it with all your might" (9:10 NASB). Diligence keeps going while frustration gives up. Diligence acts while procrastination rests. Diligence says, "I can do it" while defeat says, "I can't."

To work with diligence is essential to every facet of our spiritual and physical lives. With devoted tenacity, we seek God and His will. With steadfast determination, we pray and study His Word.

Wherever we are or whatever we do, God calls us to remain diligent—even when our greatest efforts seem vain or our hard work goes unnoticed.

Lord, I often make mistakes on the path of life, losing sight of the trail and calling out for You. Thank You for finding me, for putting my feet back on the path and leading me home. Amen.

I will remember my song in the night;
I will meditate with my heart, and my spirit ponders.
PSALM 77:6 NASB

"But be very careful to keep the commandment and the law that
Moses the servant of the LORD gave you: to love the LORD your God,
to walk in obedience to him, to keep his commands, to hold fast to
him and to serve him with all your heart and with all your soul."
JOSHUA 22:5 NIV

Keep your heart with all diligence, for out of
it spring the issues of life.
PROVERBS 4:23 NKJV

Since you excel in so many ways—in your faith, your gifted
speakers, your knowledge, your enthusiasm, and your love
from us—I want you to excel also in this gracious act of giving.
2 CORINTHIANS 8:7 NLT

*Lord, I want to be instrumental in helping my family establish a close
walk with You. Direct me daily to renew my commitment to follow
in Your steps. Thank You for being the example I need. Amen.*

The soul of the sluggard craves and gets nothing,
but the soul of the diligent is made fat.
PROVERBS 13:4 NASB

He becometh poor that dealeth with a slack hand:
but the hand of the diligent maketh rich.
PROVERBS 10:4 KJV

But as for you, brethren, do not grow weary of doing good.
2 THESSALONIANS 3:13 NASB

For this very reason, make every effort to add to your faith
goodness; and to goodness, knowledge; and to knowledge,
self-control; and to self-control, perseverance; and to perseverance,
godliness; and to godliness, mutual affection; and to mutual
affection, love. . . . Therefore, my brothers and sisters,
make every effort to confirm your calling and election.
For if you do these things, you will never stumble.
2 PETER 1:5–7, 10 NIV

Behold that which I have seen: it is good and comely for one to eat
and to drink, and to enjoy the good of all his labour that he taketh
under the sun all the days of his life, which God giveth him: for it
is his portion. Every man also to whom God hath given riches and
wealth, and hath given him power to eat thereof, and to take his
portion, and to rejoice in his labour; this is the gift of God.
ECCLESIASTES 5:18–19 KJV

If it is to encourage, then give encouragement; if it is giving,
then give generously; if it is to lead, do it diligently;
if it is to show mercy, do it cheefully.
ROMANS 12:8 NIV

*Father, I don't know how You will use my life, but I have faith in
Your promises and am always ready to do Your will. Amen.*

The plans of the diligent lead surely to plenty, but those
of everyone who is hasty, surely to poverty.
PROVERBS 21:5 NKJV

So let's not get tired of doing what is good. At just the right time
we will reap a harvest of blessing if we don't give up.
GALATIANS 6:9 NLT

Wherefore, beloved, seeing that ye look for such things, be diligent
that ye may be found of him in peace, without spot, and blameless.
2 PETER 3:14 KJV

"Whatever is commanded by the God of heaven, let it be done with
zeal for the house of the God of heaven, so that there will not
be wrath against the kingdom of the king and his sons."
EZRA 7:23 NASB

Therefore, my dear brothers and sisters, stand firm. Let nothing move you. Always give yourselves fully to the work of the Lord, because you know that your labor in the Lord is not in vain.
1 CORINTHIANS 15:58 NIV

Lord, show me the path to victory every day, because sometimes I find it hard to follow. You know every turn in the road, and I will follow You in security all the days of my life. Amen.

Much food is in the fallow ground of the poor, and for lack of justice there is waste.
PROVERBS 13:23 NKJV

Whatever your hand finds to do, do it with all your might.
ECCLESIASTES 9:10 NASB

When I stand before God at the end of my life, I would hope that I would not have a single bit of talent left, and could say, "I used everything you gave me."
ERMA BOMBECK

Discipline, Family

*D*iscipline in a Christian home consists of more than issuing commands like, "No video games until you finish your homework!" or, "Stop goofing around before someone gets hurt!"

It's easy to shout directives, but administering loving discipline takes work, thought, and persistence. To establish rules and lovingly implement them is to build structure, providing children with a sense of security. Discipline teaches kids the consequences of sin and the importance of submitting to authority.

Just as God disciplines those He loves, we discipline our children out of love. And contrary to popular thinking, a disciplined child is a happy child.

*Father, raising obedient, loving children requires me to show
gentleness and patience, not threats or harshness. I pray that
You will teach me how to soften each correction with
the same love I receive from You. Amen.*

One that ruleth well his own house, having his children in
subjection with all gravity; (For if a man know not how to rule
his own house, how shall he take care of the church of God?).
1 Timothy 3:4–5 kjv

Do not withhold correction from a child, for if you beat him
with a rod, he will not die. You shall beat him with
a rod, and deliver his soul from hell.
Proverbs 23:13–14 nkjv

Those who spare the rod of discipline hate their children.
Those who love their children care enough to discipline them.
Proverbs 13:24 nlt

Foolishness is bound in the heart of a child; but the
rod of correction shall drive it far from him.
Proverbs 22:15 kjv

Fathers, do not aggravate your children, or they
will become discouraged.
Colossians 3:21 nlt

*I can't think of anything parents could do to children
more heartless than failing to discipline.*
Janette Oke

Even small children are known by their actions,
so is their conduct really pure and upright?
PROVERBS 20:11 NIV

Fathers, do not provoke your children to anger, but bring them
up in the discipline and instruction of the Lord.
EPHESIANS 6:4 NASB

"Now behold, he has a son who has observed all his father's sins
which he committed, and observing does not do likewise. He does
not eat at the mountain shrines or lift up his eyes to the idols of
he house of Israel, or defile his neighbor's wife, or oppress anyone,
or retain a pledge, or commit robbery, but he gives his bread to
the hungry and covers the naked with clothing, he keeps his hand
from the poor, does not take interest or increase, but executes
My ordinances, and walks in My statutes; he will not
die for his father's iniquity, he will surely live."
EZEKIEL 18:14–17 NASB

*Father, help me see when my children need gentle, loving correction,
and show me the best approach. Let me be as kind and patient
with my children as You are with me. Amen.*

Discipline your children, and they will give you peace;
they will bring you the delights you desire.
PROVERBS 29:17 NIV

Discipline, God's

Ouch! Did you ever feel like God dispensed a spiritual spanking? Just as we discipline our children, our heavenly Father disciplines us. Why? Because an undisciplined life brings bondage, while a disciplined life liberates. Yes, discipline frees us.

The Lord has a good reason for everything He does, and everything He does comes from love. So rather than bemoaning the temporary pain, consider discipline's benefits: it teaches, guides, garners appreciation, gives life, establishes our spiritual "daughtership," and yields the peaceable fruit of righteousness within us.

Admit it. Discipline helps way more than it hurts!

Father, Your correction lasts only a moment, but its blessings are eternal. When I realize You are so concerned for me and want to help me, I am filled with gratitude and willing to be led in the right direction. Amen.

O Lord, do not rebuke me in Your anger,
nor chasten me in Your hot displeasure.
PSALM 6:1 NKJV

"I correct and discipline everyone I love.
So be diligent and turn from your indifference."
REVELATION 3:19 NLT

Behold, happy is the man whom God correcteth: therefore despise
not thou the chastening of the Almighty: for he maketh sore,
and bindeth up: he woundeth, and his hands make whole.
JOB 5:17–18 KJV

And you have forgotten the exhortation which is addressed to you
as sons, "MY SON, DO NOT REGARD LIGHTLY THE DISCIPLINE OF THE LORD,
NOR FAINT WHEN YOU ARE REPROVED BY HIM; FOR THOSE WHOM THE LORD
LOVES HE DISCIPLINES, AND HE SCOURGES EVERY SON WHOM HE RECEIVES."
It is for discipline that you endure; God deals with you as with
sons; for what son is there whom his father does not discipline?
But if you are without discipline, of which all have become
partakers, then you are illegitimate children and not sons.
HEBREWS 12:5–8 NASB

Know then in your heart that as a man disciplines his son,
so the LORD your God disciplines you.
DEUTERONOMY 8:5 NIV

*Father, I need to show my children how important obedience is by
being obedient myself—to You and to others in authority over
me. Thank You for assisting me in this effort. Amen.*

The LORD has punished me severely, but he did not let me die.
PSALM 118:18 NLT

For if we would judge ourselves, we would not be judged.
But when we are judged, we are chastened by the Lord,
that we may not be condemned with the world.
1 CORINTHIANS 11:31–32 NKJV

For the commandment is a lamp; and the law is light;
and reproofs of instruction are the way of life.
PROVERBS 6:23 KJV

Blessed is the man whom You chasten, O LORD, and whom You
teach out of Your law; that You may grant him relief from
the days of adversity, until a pit is dug for the wicked.
PSALM 94:12–13 NASB

For whom the LORD loves He corrects,
just as a father the son in whom he delights.
PROVERBS 3:12 NKJV

No discipline is enjoyable while it is happening—it's painful!
But afterward there will be a peaceful harvest of right
living for those who are trained in this way.
HEBREWS 12:11 NLT

*God has to punish His children from time to time
and it is the very demonstration of His love.*
ELISABETH ELLIOT

Duty

W hat is a Christian woman's duty? The scriptures list a few: to revere, serve, and obey God, and keep His commandments.

In the 1940s and '50s, a married woman's "duty" was clearly defined—to love and respect her husband while caring for her home and children. Today society has changed. God's Word, however, remains the same.

Our duty to love and respect our husbands, and care for our homes and children comes from our desire to follow biblical precepts. When we obey God and keep His commands, we automatically gain a sense of servitude toward our family and others.

What's our duty? To love God and follow His will.

Through You, Lord, I can live a life that will give others no right to accuse me of any wrongdoing. I pray that You'll allow my life to be an example that will encourage my family, friends, and others to come to You. Amen.

Let us hear the conclusion of the whole matter: Fear God,
and keep his commandments: for this is the whole duty of man.
ECCLESIASTES 12:13 KJV

"If it is disagreeable in your sight to serve the LORD, choose for
yourselves today whom you will serve: whether the gods which
your fathers served which were beyond the River, or the gods
of the Amorites in whose land you are living; but as
for me and my house, we will serve the LORD."
JOSHUA 24:15 NASB

"Now if you obey me fully and keep my covenant, then out
of all nations you will be my treasured possession.
Although the whole earth is mine."
EXODUS 19:5 NIV

"You shall therefore keep His statutes and His commandments which
I command you today, that it may go well with you and with your
children after you, and that you may prolong your days in the
land which the LORD your God is giving you for all time."
DEUTERONOMY 4:40 NKJV

When people's lives please the LORD,
even their enemies are at peace with them.
PROVERBS 16:7 NLT

"So why do you keep calling me 'Lord, Lord!'
when you don't do what I say?"
LUKE 6:46 NLT

*Lord, make me a living sacrifice for You, that I might lead others
to You. Let my praises be a godly example in my home.
I praise You with all that is within me. Amen.*

And shewing mercy unto thousands of them that love me,
and keep my commandments.
EXODUS 20:6 KJV

"Be careful to listen to all these words which I command you,
so that it may be well with you and your sons after you forever,
for you will be doing what is good and right in
the sight of the LORD your God."
DEUTERONOMY 12:28 NASB

"You will be hated by everyone because of me,
but the one who stands firm to the end will be saved."
MATTHEW 10:22 NIV

"See, I have set before you today life and good, death and evil,
in that I command you today to love the LORD your God, to walk
in His ways, and to keep His commandments, His statutes, and His
judgments, that you may live and multiply; and the LORD your
God will bless you in the land which you go to possess."
DEUTERONOMY 30:15–16 NKJV

Laziness may appear attractive, but work gives satisfaction.
ANNE FRANK

Encouragement

A little encouragement goes a long way.

It's been a bad week. You lost your car keys, burned your favorite recipe, misplaced important papers, ran late for work, and forgot a parent-teacher conference. Plus, your devotional time seems to have disappeared with those keys.

Discouraged, you enter church on Sunday fully prepared to force a fake smile. Instead, you're encouraged. The Sunday school lesson and sermon are just for you, and the fellowship is great. Instantly, your deflated optimism fades into the distant past and you are revitalized, ready to share the encouragement you received with someone else.

Lord, on days when I'm having spiritual struggles, my thoughts become full of discouragement and frustration. I don't like to be so controlled by my emotions. Please give me the strength to be pure in every situation. Amen.

You must warn each other every day, while it is still "today," so that
none of you will be deceived by sin and hardened against God.
HEBREWS 3:13 NLT

Confirming the souls of the disciples, and exhorting them to
continue in the faith, and that we must through much
tribulation enter into the kingdom of God.
ACTS 14:22 KJV

Holding fast the faithful word which is in accordance
with the teaching, so that he will be able both to exhort in
sound doctrine and to refute those who contradict.
TITUS 1:9 NASB

Not giving up meeting together, as some are in the habit
of doing, but encouraging one another—and all
the more as you see the Day approaching.
HEBREWS 10:25 NIV

I can do all things through Christ who strengthens me.
PHILIPPIANS 4:13 NKJV

*Lord, You've given me a life that abounds with rich blessings,
and You've guaranteed that because of this You also have great
expectations of me. Help me to be faithful to these expectations. Amen.*

Now if we are afflicted, it is for your consolation and salvation, which is effective for enduring the same sufferings which we also suffer. Or if we are comforted, it is for your consolation and salvation.
2 CORINTHIANS 1:6 NKJV

With all these things in mind, dear brothers and sisters, stand firm and keep a strong grip on the teaching we passed on to you both in person and by letter. Now may our Lord Jesus Christ himself and God our Father, who loved us and by his grace gave us eternal comfort and a wonderful hope, comfort you and strengthen you in every good thing you do and say.
2 THESSALONIANS 2:15–17 NLT

Therefore encourage one another and build each other up, just as in fact you are doing.
1 THESSALONIANS 5:11 NIV

Lord, help me to teach my children that to grow as encouragers, they can start with small things as they comfort others and build from there. Amen.

All Scripture is God-breathed and is useful for teaching, rebuking, correcting and training in righteousness.
2 TIMOTHY 3:16 NIV

Do not merely look out for your own personal interests, but also for the interests of others.
PHILIPPIANS 2:4 NASB

Ye are witnesses, and God also, how holily and justly and
unblameably we behaved ourselves among you that believe:
as ye know how we exhorted and comforted and charged every
one of you, as a father doth his children, that ye would walk
worthy of God, who hath called you unto his kingdom and
glory. For this cause also thank we God without ceasing,
because, when ye received the word of God which ye heard
of us, ye received it not as the word of men, but as it
is in truth, the word of God, which effectually
worketh also in you that believe.
1 THESSALONIANS 2:10–13 KJV

Share each other's burdens, and in this way obey the law of Christ.
GALATIANS 6:2 NLT

Brethren, if anyone among you wanders from the truth,
and someone turns him back, let him know that he who
turns a sinner from the error of his way will save a
soul from death and cover a multitude of sins.
JAMES 5:19–20 NKJV

"When they bring you before the synagogues and the rulers and
the authorities, do not worry about how or what you are to speak
in your defense, or what you are to say; for the Holy Spirit
will teach you in that very hour what you ought to say."
LUKE 12:11–12 NASB

*What men and women need is encouragement. . . . Instead of
always harping on a man's faults, tell him of his virtues.
Try to pull him out of his rut of bad habits.*
ELEANOR H. PORTER

Eternity

*E*arthly life is short but eternity is forever. With that in mind, we all need to stand ready to meet the Lord.

Heaven is an actual place, not some mystical golden-gated wisp of cumulus clouds topped with angels. The most majestic places, ideals, and valued treasures can't compare to what God has prepared for those who love Him. And the best part about heaven is the One who rules and reigns there.

Right now, Jesus prepares your eternal home. And one day all of life's problems and trials will vanish in the light of an eternity with Him.

Forever, Lord—what encouragement is in that word. We have all eternity to spend with You in heaven. Thank You for this indescribable gift. Thank You for being the Alpha and the Omega, the first and the last. Amen.

"There is more than enough room in my Father's home. If this were not so, would I have told you that I am going to prepare a place for you? When everything is ready, I will come and get you, so that you will always be with me where I am."
JOHN 14:2–3 NLT

In the future there is laid up for me the crown of righteousness, which the Lord, the righteous Judge, will award to me on that day; and not only to me, but also to all who have loved His appearing.
2 TIMOTHY 4:8 NASB

And I saw a new heaven and a new earth: for the first heaven and the first earth were passed away; and there was no more sea. And I John saw the holy city, new Jerusalem, coming down from God out of heaven, prepared as a bride adorned for her husband.
REVELATION 21:1–2 KJV

Jesus said to them, "You will indeed drink from my cup, but to sit at my right or left is not for me to grant. These places belong to those for whom they have been prepared by my Father."
MATTHEW 20:23 NIV

Lord, I know there will come a day when we will be in heaven with You. I look forward to that time, and I thank You for the opportunity to share that time and place with You. Amen.

"Those who love their life in this world will lose it. Those who care nothing for their life in this world will keep it for eternity."
JOHN 12:25 NLT

"And I give them eternal life, and they shall never perish;
neither shall anyone snatch them out of My hand."
JOHN 10:28 NKJV

Behold, I tell you a mystery: We shall not all sleep, but we shall all
be changed—in a moment, in the twinkling of an eye, at the last
trumpet. For the trumpet will sound, and the dead will be raised
incorruptible, and we shall be changed. For this corruptible must
put on incorruption, and this mortal must put on immortality.
So when this corruptible has put on incorruption, and this mortal
has put on immortality, then shall be brought to pass the saying
that is written: "Death is swallowed up in victory."
1 CORINTHIANS 15:51–54 NKJV

But in keeping with his promise we are looking forward to a new
heaven and a new earth, where righteousness dwells.
2 PETER 3:13 NIV

For he who sows to his flesh will of the flesh reap corruption
but he who sows to the Spirit will of the Spirit reap everlasting life.
GALATIANS 6:8 NKJV

*Father, when my time on earth comes to an end, I pray I will be able
to bear death as well as I bore life, secure in Your love and looking
to the salvation that You have promised is mine. Amen.*

And many of them that sleep in the dust of the earth shall
awake, some to everlasting life, and some to
shame and everlasting contempt.
DANIEL 12:2 KJV

Jesus said to her, "I am the resurrection and the life; he who believes in Me will live even if he dies, and everyone who lives and believes in Me will never die. Do you believe this?"
JOHN 11:25–26 NASB

"You study the Scriptures diligently because you think that in them you have eternal life. These are the very Scriptures that testify about me."
JOHN 5:39 NIV

But in accordance with your hardness and your impenitent heart you are treasuring up for yourself wrath in the day of wrath and revelation of the righteous judgment of God, who "will render to each one according to his deeds": eternal life to those who by patient continuance in doing good seek for glory, honor, and immortality.
ROMANS 2:5–7 NKJV

"But don't be so concerned about perishable things like food. Spend your energy seeking the eternal life that the Son of Man can give you. For God the Father has given me the seal of his approval."
JOHN 6:27 NLT

Lord, if I trust You for my eternal salvation, why don't I trust You for my daily needs? Instill in me the peace that comes from casting all my cares on You. Amen.

But if the Spirit of him that raised up Jesus from the dead dwell in you, he that raised up Christ from the dead shall also quicken your mortal bodies by his Spirit that dwelleth in you.
ROMANS 8:11 KJV

And when the Great Shepherd appears, you will
receive a crown of never-ending glory and honor.
1 PETER 5:4 NLT

And there will no longer be any night; and they will not have need
of the light of a lamp nor the light of the sun, because the Lord
God will illumine them; and they will reign forever and ever.
REVELATION 22:5 NASB

Therefore are they before the throne of God, and serve him day
and night in his temple: and he that sitteth on the throne shall dwell
among them. They shall hunger no more, neither thirst any more;
neither shall the sun light on them, nor any heat. For the Lamb
which is in the midst of the throne shall feed them, and shall
lead them unto living fountains of waters: and God
shall wipe away all tears from their eyes.
REVELATION 7:15–17 KJV

All praise to God, the Father of our Lord Jesus Christ. It is by his
great mercy that we have been born again, because God raised Jesus
Christ from the dead. Now we live with great expectation, and we
have a priceless inheritance—an inheritance that is kept in heaven
for you, pure and undefiled, beyond the reach of change and
decay. And through your faith, God is protecting you by
his power until you receive this salvation, which is
ready to be revealed on the last day for all to see.
1 PETER 1:3–5 NLT

Redeemed, how I love to proclaim it!
His child, and forever, I am.
FANNIE CROSBY

Faith

*Y*ou may be unaware of it, but you exercise faith daily. By faith you fall asleep, confident of morning. You eat, expecting nourishment. You breathe in air you can't see. You drive your car, trusting it will take you to your destination.

Jesus said that faith as tiny as a mustard seed is enough to produce miraculous results. So why do we assume that only mountain-moving faith will do? The Word of God is a faith-builder. So read on and cause that mustard seed to flourish and grow.

Lord, keep me strong in my faith, no matter what. When I am following You, I can be blessed, no matter what others say about me. Thank You, Jesus, for mapping the way for me. Amen.

But he must ask in faith without any doubting, for the one who doubts is like the surf of the sea, driven and tossed by the wind.
JAMES 1:6 NASB

He replied, "If you have faith as small as a mustard seed, you can say to this mulberry tree, 'Be uprooted and planted in the sea,' and it will obey you."
LUKE 17:6 NIV

Whom having not seen you love. Though now you do not see Him, yet believing, you rejoice with joy inexpressible and full of glory.
1 PETER 1:8 NKJV

But Jesus overheard them and said to Jairus,
"Don't be afraid. Just have faith."
MARK 5:36 NLT

And he said to the woman, Thy faith hath saved thee; go in peace.
LUKE 7:50 KJV

Lord, my faith seems weak—not the type of faith that might bring victory. But in You I have the assurance of victory. I've read the story, and in the end You will reign victorious. I praise You, Lord. Amen.

For you are all sons of God through faith in Christ Jesus.
GALATIANS 3:26 NASB

Yet to all who did receive him, to those who believed in his name, he gave the right to become children of God.
JOHN 1:12 NIV

And Jesus said to him, " 'If You can?'
All things are possible to him who believes."
MARK 9:23 NASB

That Christ may dwell in your hearts by faith; that ye, being rooted
and grounded in love, may be able to comprehend with all saints
what is the breadth, and length, and depth, and height; and to
know the love of Christ, which passeth knowledge,
that ye might be filled with all the fulness of God.
EPHESIANS 3:17–19 KJV

"It is written in the Prophets: 'They will all be taught by God.'
Everyone who has heard the Father and learned
from him comes to me."
JOHN 6:45 NIV

*I often feel that I lack faith, Lord, that You must be speaking promises
for someone else—someone more faithful and deserving of
them. Show me the error of this thinking. Amen.*

That your faith should not be in the wisdom
of men but in the power of God.
1 CORINTHIANS 2:5 NKJV

That if thou shalt confess with thy mouth the Lord Jesus,
and shalt believe in thine heart that God hath raised
him from the dead, thou shalt be saved.
ROMANS 10:9 KJV

Jesus said to him, "Thomas, because you have seen Me, you have
believed. Blessed are those who have not seen and yet have believed."
JOHN 20:29 NKJV

And it is impossible to please God without faith. Anyone who
wants to come to him must believe that God exists and
that he rewards those who sincerely seek him.
HEBREWS 11:6 NLT

*Lord, when times are hard and I become discouraged, be with me.
Keep me a faithful teacher of the Way for the sake of
my children and all those to come. Amen.*

For we walk by faith, not by sight.
2 CORINTHIANS 5:7 KJV

Jesus answered and said to them, "This is the work of God,
that you believe in Him whom He has sent."
JOHN 6:29 NASB

"Behold, I stand at the door and knock. If anyone hears My
voice and opens the door, I will come in to him
and dine with him, and he with Me."
REVELATION 3:20 NKJV

*Father, give me faithfulness in all things large and small, so that
I may be an example to my children and a blessing to my
husband—and to all those near me. Amen.*

Let us draw near with a sincere heart in full assurance of faith,
having our hearts sprinkled clean from an evil conscience
and our bodies washed with pure water.
HEBREWS 10:22 NASB

Jesus saith unto her, Said I not unto thee, that, if thou wouldest
believe, thou shouldest see the glory of God?
JOHN 11:40 KJV

I have been crucified with Christ; and it is no longer I who
live, but Christ lives in me; and the life which I now
live in the flesh I live by faith in the Son of God,
who loved me and gave Himself up for me.
GALATIANS 2:20 NASB

Be on guard. Stand firm in the faith. Be courageous. Be strong.
1 CORINTHIANS 16:13 NLT

Whoever believes in the Son of God accepts this testimony.
Whoever does not believe God has made him out to be
a liar, because they have not believed the testimony
God has given about his Son.
1 JOHN 5:10 NIV

And now, just as you accepted Christ Jesus as your Lord, you must
continue to follow him. Let your roots grow down into him, and let
your lives be built on him. Then your faith will grow strong in the
truth you were taught, and you will overflow with thankfulness.
COLOSSIANS 2:6–7 NLT

*Faith sees the invisible, believes the unbelievable,
and receives the impossible.*
CORRIE TEN BOOM

Faithfulness of God

*I*t's a fact. Even the most dependable people fail us: our husbands, our parents, our friends. They don't mean to—they're only human just as we are. On the other hand, we can fully depend on God's faithfulness at all times.

What God says, He does. His promises are true. What He did for His people and the prophets of old, He does for us today. We can safely trust Him at His Word whatever the circumstance. Always remember: God cannot lie, and His faithfulness endures forever.

It's a fact!

Father, when troubles come, I never have to face them alone. Thank You for always being with me as my refuge and strength. When all else fails, I put my trust in You and am never disappointed. Amen.

And we know that in all things God works for the good of those who love him, who have been called according to his purpose.
ROMANS 8:28 NIV

And the heavens will praise Your wonders, O LORD; Your faithfulness also in the assembly of the saints.
PSALM 89:5 NKJV

The trustworthy person will get a rich reward, but a person who wants quick riches will get into trouble.
PROVERBS 28:20 NLT

In hope of eternal life, which God, that cannot lie, promised before the world began.
TITUS 1:2 KJV

"Who then is the faithful and sensible slave whom his master put in charge of his household to give them their food at the proper time? Blessed is that slave whom his master finds so doing when he comes. Truly I say to you that he will put him in charge of all his possessions."
MATTHEW 24:45–47 NASB

Lord, the next time I am faced with danger for Your sake, let me remember that You are faithful to reward Your people, no matter how much I may fear. Amen.

So this is what the Sovereign LORD says: "See, I lay a stone in Zion, a tested stone, a precious cornerstone for a sure foundation; the one who relies on it will never be stricken with panic."
ISAIAH 28:16 NIV

(For the LORD thy God is a merciful God;) he will not forsake
thee, neither destroy thee, nor forget the covenant
of thy fathers which he sware unto them.
DEUTERONOMY 4:31 KJV

Let us hold fast the confession of our hope without
wavering, for He who promised is faithful.
HEBREWS 10:23 NASB

If we are faithless, He remains faithful;
He cannot deny Himself.
2 TIMOTHY 2:13 NKJV

"God is not a man, that He should lie, nor a son of man,
that He should repent. Has He said, and will He not do?
Or has He spoken, and will He not make it good?"
NUMBERS 23:19 NKJV

*Father, the life I am living right now is not the result of my faith
in You but of Your faith in me. Thank You for Your sacrifice
that saves me and makes me whole. Amen.*

"Praise the LORD who has given rest to his people Israel, just as he
promised. Not one word has failed of all the wonderful
promises he gave through his servant Moses."
1 KINGS 8:56 NLT

O love the LORD, all ye his saints: for the LORD preserveth the
faithful, and plentifully rewardeth the proud doer.
PSALM 31:23 KJV

"Know therefore that the LORD your God, He is God, the faithful
God, who keeps His covenant and His lovingkindness to
a thousandth generation with those who love Him
and keep His commandments."
DEUTERONOMY 7:9 NASB

"Do not be afraid of what you are about to suffer. I tell you, the
devil will put some of you in prison to test you, and you will
suffer persecution for ten days. Be faithful, even to the point
of death, and I will give you life as your victor's crown."
REVELATION 2:10 NIV

The Lord isn't really being slow about his promise, as some people
think. No, he is being patient for your sake. He does not want
anyone to be destroyed, but wants everyone to repent.
2 PETER 3:9 NLT

*God's designs regarding you, and His methods of bringing
about these designs, are infinitely wise.*
MADAME GUYON

Fearing God

*F*ear God? Aren't we supposed to trust, not fear the Lord? Fear isn't of God, right?

In the following verses we discover the definition of "fearing" God, and it's not what some people might think. The word *fear* is derived from the Greek word *eulabeia,* signifying caution and reverence.

When a godly fear and love are combined, they constitute a heartfelt devotion toward God. To fear the Lord is to reverence, love, respect, and honor Him. There's nothing scary about that!

Lord, I want my heart to continually be filled with praise and thanksgiving to You. Keep me anchored in the thought that all You do is for my good and glory. Only You are deserving of my praise and adoration. Amen.

"Do not be afraid of those who kill the body but cannot kill
the soul. Rather, be afraid of the One who can
destroy both soul and body in hell."
MATTHEW 10:28 NIV

"Moreover you shall select from all the people able men, such as
fear God, men of truth, hating covetousness; and place
such over them to be rulers of thousands, rulers of
hundreds, rulers of fifties, and rulers of tens."
EXODUS 18:21 NKJV

Fear of the LORD is the foundation of true knowledge,
but fools despise wisdom and discipline.
PROVERBS 1:7 NLT

Saying with a loud voice, Fear God, and give glory to him; for the
hour of his judgment is come: and worship him that made heaven,
and earth, and the sea, and the fountains of waters.
REVELATION 14:7 KJV

"Oh that they had such a heart in them, that they would fear
Me and keep all My commandments always, that it may
be well with them and with their sons forever!"
DEUTERONOMY 5:29 NASB

The angel of the LORD encamps around those
who fear him, and he delivers them.
PSALM 34:7 NIV

Precious Father, on my own, I am bound to fail. Now that I have put my trust in You, I cannot fail, for You are always the victor, and this knowledge makes me strong where once I was weak. Amen.

A wise man feareth, and departeth from evil:
but the fool rageth, and is confident.
PROVERBS 14:16 KJV

Therefore, since we receive a kingdom which cannot be shaken,
let us show gratitude, by which we may offer to God an acceptable
service with reverence and awe; for our God is a consuming fire.
HEBREWS 12:28–29 NASB

"Therefore, people revere him, for does he not
have regard for all the wise in heart?"
JOB 37:24 NIV

Serve the LORD with fear, and rejoice with trembling.
PSALM 2:11 KJV

He will fulfil the desire of them that fear him:
he also will hear their cry, and will save them.
PSALM 145:19 KJV

Father, I ask for Your wisdom and guidance. Instruct me in the best ways to teach my children about Your great love. I trust You will guide me so I may serve You all the days of my life. Amen.

Because we have these promises, dear friends, let us cleanse
ourselves from everything that can defile our body or spirit.
And let us work toward complete holiness because we fear God.
2 CORINTHIANS 7:1 NLT

The secret of the LORD is with those who fear Him,
and He will show them His covenant.
PSALM 25:14 NKJV

"Have you no respect for me? Why don't you tremble in my
presence? I, the LORD, define the ocean's sandy shoreline as an
everlasting boundary that the waters cannot cross. The waves may
toss and roar, but they can never pass the boundaries I set."
JEREMIAH 5:22 NLT

Therefore, my beloved, as you have always obeyed,
not as in my presence only, but now much more in my absence,
work out your own salvation with fear and trembling.
PHILIPPIANS 2:12 NKJV

Then those who feared the LORD spoke to one another, and the LORD
gave attention and heard it, and a book of remembrance was written
before Him for those who fear the LORD and who esteem His name.
MALACHI 3:16 NASB

Reverence for the Lord is the beginning of wisdom.
ELISABETH ELLIOT

Forgiveness

*H*ow do we forgive someone who has wronged us or hurt someone we love? How can we forgive when we don't feel forgiveness?

Corrie ten Boom, survivor of a women's Nazi concentration camp, wrote: "Forgiveness is an act of the will, and the will can function regardless of the temperature of the heart."

For every Christian, forgiveness is a choice. In order to fully receive God's forgiveness, we must willingly extend forgiveness to others.

Through an act of her will, Corrie forgave her persecutors and her sister's murderers. Jesus forgave humankind of even more. How can we do less?

Lord, give me the strength to forgive others so You will forgive me my own trespasses. Amen.

Be kind and compassionate to one another, forgiving each other,
just as in Christ God forgave you.
EPHESIANS 4:32 NIV

Bearing with one another, and forgiving one another, if anyone
has a complaint against another; even as Christ
forgave you, so you also must do.
COLOSSIANS 3:13 NKJV

Don't repay evil for evil. Don't retaliate with insults when people
insult you. Instead, pay them back with a blessing. That is what
God has called you to do, and he will grant you his blessing.
1 PETER 3:9 NLT

For if ye forgive men their trespasses, your heavenly Father will
also forgive you: but if ye forgive not men their trespasses,
neither will your Father forgive your trespasses.
MATTHEW 6:14–15 KJV

Then Peter came and said to Him, "Lord, how often shall my
brother sin against me and I forgive him? Up to seven times?"
Jesus said to him, "I do not say to you, up to seven
times, but up to seventy times seven."
MATTHEW 18:21–22 NASB

"Forgive us our debts, as we also have forgiven our debtors."
MATTHEW 6:12 NIV

Father, show me the way to true forgiveness. I want to do Your will despite my weakness. Be my guide along this difficult path that leads to my own sorely needed forgiveness. Amen.

O Lord, you are so good, so ready to forgive,
so full of unfailing love for all who ask for your help.
PSALM 86:5 NLT

And forgive us our sins; for we also forgive every one
that is indebted to us. And lead us not into
temptation; but deliver us from evil.
LUKE 11:4 KJV

"But I say to you, do not resist an evil person; but whoever slaps
you on your right cheek, turn the other to him also. If anyone
wants to sue you and take your shirt, let him have your coat
also. Whoever forces you to go one mile, go with him two."
MATTHEW 5:39–41 NASB

"If My people who are called by My name will humble themselves,
and pray and seek My face, and turn from their wicked ways,
then I will hear from heaven, and will forgive
their sin and heal their land."
2 CHRONICLES 7:14 NKJV

Father, when I am a poor example to someone I meet, grant me forgiveness. Grant those I offend the wisdom to understand that no one is free of sin, but Your grace is sufficient. Amen.

76

So watch yourselves. "If your brother or sister sins against you, rebuke them; and if they repent, forgive them. Even if they sin against you seven times in a day and seven times come back to you saying, 'I repent,' you must forgive them."

Luke 17:3–4 NIV

Judge not, and ye shall not be judged: condemn not, and ye shall not be condemned: forgive, and ye shall be forgiven.

Luke 6:37 KJV

Turning toward the woman, He said to Simon, "Do you see this woman? I entered your house; you gave Me no water for My feet, but she has wet My feet with her tears and wiped them with her hair. You gave Me no kiss; but she, since the time I came in, has not ceased to kiss My feet. You did not anoint My head with oil, but she anointed My feet with perfume. For this reason I say to you, her sins, which are many, have been forgiven, for she loved much; but he who is forgiven little, loves little."
Then He said to her, "Your sins have been forgiven."

Luke 7:44–48 NASB

If the wounds of millions are to be healed,
what other way is there except through forgiveness?

Catherine Marshall

Friendship

*S*ociety uses the term friendship loosely. Social networking websites like Facebook connect us with scores of "friends" simultaneously—yet many of them are only acquaintances, not true friends.

The following passages unveil the meaning of a true friend. She's someone who brings out the best in you, who loves and gives unselfishly. She listens and speaks the truth with kindness—and when others criticize you, she stands in your defense.

Friendship is never one-sided, because to have a friend, we must be a friend. Think of your very best girlfriend. Does she reflect the attributes of a true friend? Do you?

Lord, I thank You for my friends—for the women in my life whom I can talk to and who understand what I'm going through. Help me to be a true friend to these women you've blessed me with. Amen.

As iron sharpens iron, so one person sharpens another.
PROVERBS 27:17 NIV

And He said to them, "Which of you shall have a friend, and go
to him at midnight and say to him, 'Friend, lend me three loaves;
for a friend of mine has come to me on his journey, and I have
nothing to set before him'; and he will answer from within and say,
'Do not trouble me; the door is now shut, and my children are with
me in bed; I cannot rise and give to you'? I say to you, though he
will not rise and give to him because he is his friend, yet because of
his persistence he will rise and give him as many as he needs."
LUKE 11:5–8 NKJV

A friend is always loyal, and a brother
is born to help in time of need.
PROVERBS 17:17 NLT

A man that hath friends must shew himself friendly:
and there is a friend that sticketh closer than a brother.
PROVERBS 18:24 KJV

"For the despairing man there should be kindness from his friend;
so that he does not forsake the fear of the Almighty."
JOB 6:14 NASB

My friends are my estate.
EMILY DICKINSON

Generosity

*E*ach Thanksgiving, Phyllis opens her home to the widows and singles of her church. She spends hours in meal preparations and sets the table with her finest china and best linens. Becky spends eight hours each week babysitting for young moms in need of a break. And for years, Lori and Esther have visited a local nursing home, sharing small gifts and homemade cookies with the residents.

Displays of generosity are as varied and numerous as the human fingerprint. Giving of our time, money, or talents is generous because we are giving of ourselves.

Lord, help me to be as generous. Give me Your guidance. Reveal the needs of my brother and sister—whether they are physical, emotional, or spiritual—and incline my heart to them. Amen.

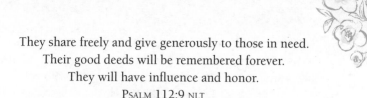

They share freely and give generously to those in need.
Their good deeds will be remembered forever.
They will have influence and honor.
PSALM 112:9 NLT

Do not withhold good from those to whom it is due,
when it is in your power to act. Do not say to your neighbor,
"Come back tomorrow and I'll give it to you"—
when you already have it with you.
PROVERBS 3:27–28 NIV

He answered and said to them, "He who has two tunics, let him give
to him who has none; and he who has food, let him do likewise."
LUKE 3:11 NKJV

"When you give to someone in need, don't do as the hypocrites
do—blowing trumpets in the synagogues and streets to call
attention to their acts of charity! I tell you the truth, they have
received all the reward they will ever get. But when you give
to someone in need, don't let your left hand know what your
right hand is doing. Give your gifts in private, and your
Father, who sees everything, will reward you."
MATTHEW 6:2–4 NLT

Lord, You promise me wonderful rewards when I am charitable.
But I cannot answer every request made of me, so I count on
You to guide me as to where I should invest my efforts
in such a way as to bring You glory. Amen.

He that despiseth his neighbour sinneth: but he
that hath mercy on the poor, happy is he.
PROVERBS 14:21 KJV

"Now in case a countryman of yours becomes poor and his
means with regard to you falter, then you are to sustain him,
like a stranger or a sojourner, that he may live with you."
LEVITICUS 25:35 NASB

If any woman who is a believer has widows in her care, she should
continue to help them and not let the church be burdened
with them, so that the church can help those
widows who are really in need.
1 TIMOTHY 5:16 NIV

And He saw also a certain poor widow putting in two mites.
So He said, "Truly I say to you that this poor widow has put
in more than all; for all these out of their abundance have
put in offerings for God, but she out of her poverty
put in all the livelihood that she had."
LUKE 21:2–4 NKJV

"There will always be some in the land who are poor. That is
why I am commanding you to share freely with
the poor and with other Israelites in need."
DEUTERONOMY 15:11 NLT

If a brother or sister be naked, and destitute of daily food, and one
of you say unto them, Depart in peace, be ye warmed and filled;
notwithstanding ye give them not those things which
are needful to the body; what doth it profit?
JAMES 2:15–16 KJV

*Lord Jesus, draw my family close to You. Fill our home with Your
presence and our lives with Your love. In turn, help each one
of us to realize the importance of blessing others. Amen.*

How blessed is he who considers the helpless; the Lord will deliver him in a day of trouble. The Lord will protect him and keep him alive, and he shall be called blessed upon the earth; and do not give him over to the desire of his enemies.

PSALM 41:1–2 NASB

Each of you should give what you have decided in your heart to give, not reluctantly or under compulsion, for God loves a cheerful giver.

2 CORINTHIANS 9:7 NIV

For whosoever shall give you a cup of water to drink in my name, because ye belong to Christ, verily I say unto you, he shall not lose his reward.

MARK 9:41 KJV

"Then the King will say to those on His right hand, 'Come, you blessed of My Father, inherit the kingdom prepared for you from the foundation of the world: for I was hungry and you gave Me food; I was thirsty and you gave Me drink; I was a stranger and you took Me in; I was naked and you clothed Me; I was sick and you visited Me; I was in prison and you came to Me.' Then the righteous will answer Him, saying, 'Lord, when did we see You hungry and feed You, or thirsty and give You drink? When did we see You a stranger and take You in, or naked and clothe You? Or when did we see You sick, or in prison, and come to You?' And the King will answer and say to them, 'Assuredly, I say to you, inasmuch as you did it to one of the least of these My brethren, you did it to Me.'"

MATTHEW 25:34–40 NKJV

"Share your food with the hungry, and give shelter to the homeless.
Give clothes to those who need them, and do not hide from
relatives who need your help. Then your salvation will
come like the dawn, and your wounds will quickly heal.
Your godliness will lead you forward, and the glory
of the Lord will protect you from behind."
Isaiah 58:7–8 NLT

*Lord, show me how to be a godly woman, how to have true contentment
that comes from service to You. Help me to reinforce in my home the
need to be satisfied with doing Your will. Amen.*

"Give, and it will be given to you: good measure, pressed down,
shaken together, and running over will be put into your
bosom. For with the same measure that you
use, it will be measured back to you."
Luke 6:38 NKJV

If you help the poor, you are lending to
the Lord—and he will repay you!
Proverbs 19:17 NLT

I have shewed you all things, how that so labouring ye ought to
support the weak, and to remember the words of the Lord Jesus,
how he said, It is more blessed to give than to receive.
Acts 20:35 KJV

It's not how much we give but how much love we put into giving.
Mother Teresa

Gentleness

*D*r. James Dobson, Christian psychologist and author, recalls the gentleness his wife exhibited whenever she awakened their then-small daughter from a nap. Standing nearby, Dobson would watch as Shirley gently stirred their child from slumber with her soft, sweet, soothing words. Her genteel manner impacted the renowned psychologist so much that he spoke of it many years later.

How we approach people matters. Are we brazen and critical? Or are we compassionate, seasoning our words with kindness? Gentleness is a fruit of the Spirit that brings much-needed relief in a harsh world.

Lord, direct me daily to accept and apply the strength that You've offered, so that I will truly have the gentle spirit that You intended me to have. Thank You, Jesus, that I don't have to do this on my own. Amen.

"Take My yoke upon you and learn from Me, for I am gentle
and humble in heart, and YOU WILL FIND REST FOR YOUR SOULS."
MATTHEW 11:29 NASB

But the meek will inherit the land and enjoy peace and prosperity.
PSALM 37:11 NIV

Now I, Paul, myself am pleading with you by the meekness
and gentleness of Christ—who in presence am lowly
among you, but being absent am bold toward you.
2 CORINTHIANS 10:1 NKJV

Remind the believers to submit to the government and its
officers. They should be obedient, always ready to do what is good.
They must not slander anyone and must avoid quarreling. Instead,
they should be gentle and show true humility to everyone.
TITUS 3:1–2 NLT

*Father, help me understand faithfulness and to trust in Your love above
all else, claiming none of Your glory as a personal reward. Amen.*

The LORD sustains the humble but casts the wicked to the ground.
PSALM 147:6 NIV

He tends his flock like a shepherd: He gathers the lambs
in his arms and carries them close to his heart;
he gently leads those that have young.
ISAIAH 40:11 NIV

He leads the humble in justice, and He teaches the humble His way.
PSALM 25:9 NASB

*Father, You gave me my children to cherish, and that includes being
gentle with them. I do treasure them, Lord, so help me
to impart Your gentleness to them. Amen.*

But the fruit of the Spirit is love, joy, peace,
longsuffering, gentleness, goodness, faith.
GALATIANS 5:22 KJV

But the wisdom from above is first pure, then peaceable,
gentle, reasonable, full of mercy and good fruits,
unwavering, without hypocrisy.
JAMES 3:17 NASB

As apostles of Christ we certainly had a right to make some
demands of you, but instead we were like children among you.
Or we were like a mother feeding and caring for her own children.
1 THESSALONIANS 2:7 NLT

"You have also given me the shield of Your salvation;
your gentleness has made me great."
2 SAMUEL 22:36 NKJV

For the LORD taketh pleasure in his people:
he will beautify the meek with salvation.
PSALM 149:4 KJV

*Take my heart and make it your dwelling place so
that everyone I touch will be touched also by you!*
ALICE JOYCE DAVIDSON

God's Love

*H*ave you ever read 1 Corinthians 13—the "Love Chapter"? The Living Bible says that love is patient and kind; never boastful, selfish, or rude. Love never demands its own way or is glad about injustice—rather, love rejoices when the truth wins out. Love is loyal no matter the cost. Love always believes the best in us and stands its ground in defending us.

Now substitute the word *love* with "God" and read that paragraph again. You see, God not only loves—He *is* love. No other love in heaven or on earth compares to God's because His very nature defines *agape*—selfless, unconditional—love. And that's how God loves us.

Thank You, Jesus, for Your sacrificial love for me. Thank You for the example of true love that You have provided. Amen.

Behold, what manner of love the Father hath bestowed
upon us, that we should be called the sons of God.
1 JOHN 3:1 KJV

By this the love of God was manifested in us, that God has
sent His only begotten Son into the world so
that we might live through Him.
1 JOHN 4:9 NASB

"I will heal their waywardness and love them freely,
for my anger has turned away from them."
HOSEA 14:4 NIV

But as it is written: "Eye has not seen, nor ear heard,
nor have entered into the heart of man the things
which God has prepared for those who love Him."
1 CORINTHIANS 2:9 NKJV

The LORD preserves all who love Him,
but all the wicked He will destroy.
PSALM 145:20 NKJV

And I am convinced that nothing can ever separate us from
God's love. Neither death nor life, neither angels nor demons,
neither our fears for today nor our worries about tomorrow—
not even the powers of hell can separate us from God's love.
No power in the sky above or in the earth below—indeed,
nothing in all creation will ever be able to separate us from
the love of God that is revealed in Christ Jesus our Lord.
ROMANS 8:38–39 NLT

Forgive me, Lord, for those times when I've doubted Your love.
Let me close my eyes, hold out my hand, and know that You
are there. Thank You for being with me, Father. Amen.

And hope maketh not ashamed; because the love of God is shed
abroad in our hearts by the Holy Ghost which is given unto us.
ROMANS 5:5 KJV

"For this is how God loved the world: He gave his
one and only Son, so that everyone who believes
in him will not perish but have eternal life."
JOHN 3:16 NLT

But God commendeth his love toward us, in that,
while we were yet sinners, Christ died for us.
ROMANS 5:8 KJV

"For the Father Himself loves you, because you have loved
Me and have believed that I came forth from the Father."
JOHN 16:27 NASB

Love has its source in God,
for love is the very essence of His being.
KAY ARTHUR

God's Provision

*I*n recent years, a failing economy has caused much distress. People have lost their jobs and homes, and parents wonder how they will support their families. Yet it doesn't take a job loss to experience a financial drain, resulting in a shortage of basic necessities.

The following scriptures encourage us with words of hope and promise. Every Christian has the assurance of God's provision during tough times. As we wisely manage our money and trust in His promises, the Lord supplies—perhaps not our wants—but every one of our needs.

Thank You, Father, for giving us all the things we need for life and godliness. You are the Great Provider. Amen.

And my God shall supply all your need according
to His riches in glory by Christ Jesus.
PHILIPPIANS 4:19 NKJV

"For this reason I say to you, do not be worried about your life,
as to what you will eat or what you will drink; nor for your body,
as to what you will put on. Is not life more than food, and the body
more than clothing? Look at the birds of the air, that they do not
sow, nor reap nor gather into barns, and yet your heavenly Father
feeds them. Are you not worth much more than they? And who of
you by being worried can add a single hour to his life? And why
are you worried about clothing? Observe how the lilies of the field
grow; they do not toil nor do they spin, yet I say to you that not even
Solomon in all his glory clothed himself like one of these. But if God
so clothes the grass of the field, which is alive today and tomorrow is
thrown into the furnace, will He not much more clothe you?
You of little faith! Do not worry then, saying, 'What will we eat?'
or 'What will we drink?' or 'What will we wear for clothing?'
For the Gentiles eagerly seek all these things; for your heavenly
Father knows that you need all these things. But seek
first His kingdom and His righteousness, and all
these things will be added to you."
MATTHEW 6:25–33 NASB

The lions may grow weak and hungry,
but those who seek the LORD lack no good thing.
PSALM 34:10 NIV

He gives food to those who fear him;
he always remembers his covenant.
PSALM 111:5 NLT

*Father, I welcome Your help. You know what I need, and I
trust Your provision, knowing You always act in my best
interests and want me to have a happy life. Amen.*

Charge them that are rich in this world, that they be not
highminded, nor trust in uncertain riches, but in the
living God, who giveth us richly all things to enjoy.
1 TIMOTHY 6:17 KJV

Once I was young, and now I am old. Yet I have never seen
the godly abandoned or their children begging for bread.
PSALM 37:25 NLT

*Lift up your eyes. Your heavenly Father waits to bless you
in inconceivable ways to make your life what
you never dreamed it could be.*
ANNE ORTLUND

Gratitude

*E*vangelist Joyce Meyer has said, "Christians need an attitude of gratitude!"

Though we know that God frowns on murmuring and complaining, we do it anyway. We grumble about long stoplights, difficult neighbors, the weather, our jobs, family members, or household chores. Instead of thanking God for our blessings, we approach life with resignation rather than anticipation and gratefulness.

But what if we adjusted our attitude? We might just be happy! God's Word motivates us to discover and maintain a thankful spirit. Try it! Seize an attitude of gratitude.

Father, thank You for all You have given me, for all You have taught me, and for all the good times still to come. Amen.

Then he took the cup, and when he had given thanks,
he gave it to them saying, "Drink from it, all of you."
MATTHEW 26:27 NIV

I will praise You, O LORD, with my whole heart; I will tell of
all Your marvelous works. I will be glad and rejoice in
You; I will sing praise to Your name, O Most High.
PSALM 9:1–2 NKJV

Singing a song of thanksgiving and telling of all your wonders.
PSALM 26:7 NLT

Blessed be the LORD, that hath given rest unto his people Israel,
according to all that he promised: there hath not failed one
word of all his good promise, which he promised
by the hand of Moses his servant.
1 KINGS 8:56 KJV

O LORD, You have brought up my soul from Sheol; You have
kept me alive, that I would not go down to the pit.
PSALM 30:3 NASB

Blessed be the Lord, who daily loads us with benefits,
the God of our salvation! Selah.
PSALM 68:19 NKJV

*Father, thanks to You I get to start over, fresh and clean, because You
have made me a new person. I now have a lifetime of new days to spend
any way I choose. Thank You for Your never-ending forgiveness. Amen.*

Whoever regards one day as special does so to the Lord.
Whoever eats meat does so to the Lord, for they give
thanks to God; and whoever abstains does so to
the Lord and gives thanks to God.
ROMANS 14:6 NIV

And they, continuing daily with one accord in the temple,
and breaking bread from house to house, did eat their meat
with gladness and singleness of heart, praising God,
and having favour with all the people. And the Lord
added to the church daily such as should be saved.
ACTS 2:46–47 KJV

Many, O LORD my God, are the wonders which You have done,
and Your thoughts toward us; there is none to compare
with You. If I would declare and speak of them,
they would be too numerous to count.
PSALM 40:5 NASB

I will tell of the kindnesses of the LORD, the deeds for which he is
to be praised, according to all the LORD has done for us—yes,
the many good things he has done for the house of Israel,
according to his compassion and many kindnesses.
ISAIAH 63:7 NIV

*Thank You for dealing with my sins so thoroughly, Lord—for
granting me a new start every day and proclaiming
that I am worth saving. Amen.*

"I thank and praise you, God of my ancestors, for you have given me wisdom and strength. You have told me what we asked of you and revealed to us what the king demanded."
DANIEL 2:23 NLT

Give thanks to the LORD, for He is good,
for His lovingkindness is everlasting.
PSALM 136:1 NASB

Then he took the seven loaves and the fish, and when he had given thanks, he broke them and gave them to the disciples, and they in turn to the people.
MATTHEW 15:36 NIV

In every thing give thanks: for this is the will of God in Christ Jesus concerning you.
1 THESSALONIANS 5:18 KJV

It is good to give thanks to the LORD, and to sing praises to Your name, O Most High; to declare Your lovingkindness in the morning, and Your faithfulness every night.
PSALM 92:1–2 NKJV

*Simple gratitude helps us experience God
at work in every moment of every day.*
HARRIET CROSBY

Honesty

*T*he cashier gives you too much money in change. Do you tell her? Out-of-town friends call unexpectedly and ask to stop by. Your house is a mess, you're dead tired, and you're in your pajamas. What do you say?

These scenarios happen all the time, giving us an opportunity to shine with honesty or dim with deceit. God's Word tells us to be aboveboard and upright in our dealings with others.

The old adage says, "Honesty is the best policy." Yet it's more than that. Honesty is a way of life.

Lord, guide me daily to commit to being truthful. I know I can't expect my family to be honest if I'm not willing to set the example. Help me as I strive to be like You. Amen.

And now, dear brothers and sisters, one final thing. Fix your thoughts on what is true, and honorable, and right, and pure, and lovely, and admirable. Think about things that are excellent and worthy of praise.
PHILIPPIANS 4:8 NLT

Servants, obey in all things your masters according to the flesh; not with eyeservice, as menpleasers; but in singleness of heart, fearing God.
COLOSSIANS 3:22 KJV

"You shall not steal, nor deal falsely, nor lie to one another."
LEVITICUS 19:11 NASB

The night is nearly over; the day is almost here. So let us put aside the deeds of darkness and put on the armor of light. Let us behave decently, as in the daytime, not in carousing and drunkenness, not in sexual immorality and debauchery, not in dissension and jealousy.
ROMANS 13:12–13 NIV

Pray for us; for we are confident that we have a good conscience, in all things desiring to live honorably.
HEBREWS 13:18 NKJV

Lord, I know I am Your representative here on earth and should give no one the opportunity to reject You because of my actions. When I am within seconds of being a bad example, send me Your peace. Amen.

Make it your goal to live a quiet life, minding your own business
and working with your hands, just as we instructed you before.
Then people who are not believers will respect the way
you live, and you will not need to depend on others.
1 Thessalonians 4:11–12 nlt

Be of the same mind one toward another. . . . Recompense to no
man evil for evil. Provide things honest in the sight of all men.
Romans 12:16–17 kjv

Do not lie to one another, since you laid aside the old self with
its evil practices, and have put on the new self who is
being renewed to a true knowledge according to
the image of the One who created him.
Colossians 3:9–10 nasb

For we are taking pains to do what is right, not only in
the eyes of the Lord but also in the eyes of man.
2 Corinthians 8:21 niv

He who does not put out his money at usury, nor does he
take a bribe against the innocent. He who does
these things shall never be moved.
Psalm 15:5 nkjv

Thank You, God, for Your Word. It instructs me how to live. It brings
joy to my days and gives me strength when I am weak. Amen.

"Because of this, I always try to maintain a clear
conscience before God and all people."
ACTS 24:16 NLT

"I will maintain my innocence and never let go of it;
my conscience will not reproach me as long as I live."
JOB 27:6 NIV

Thou knowest the commandments, Do not commit adultery,
Do not kill, Do not steal, Do not bear false witness.
MARK 10:19 KJV

He that hath clean hands, and a pure heart; who hath not
lifted up his soul unto vanity, nor sworn deceitfully.
PSALM 24:4 KJV

Make room for us in your hearts; we wronged no one,
we corrupted no one, we took advantage of no one.
2 CORINTHIANS 7:2 NASB

I am Your ambassador, Lord, and every day I try to show Your
love to those who do not know You. I pray that when
the time comes, You will find me worthy. Amen.

He who walks righteously and speaks with sincerity, he who rejects
unjust gain and shakes his hands so that they hold no bribe; he who
stops his ears from hearing about bloodshed and shuts his eyes
from looking upon evil; he will dwell on the heights,
his refuge will be the impregnable rock; his bread
will be given him, his water will be sure.
ISAIAH 33:15–16 NASB

Even corrupt tax collectors came to be baptized and
asked, "Teacher, what should we do?" He replied,
"Collect no more taxes than the government requires."
LUKE 3:12–13 NLT

Do not do what you would undo if caught.
LEAH ARENDT

Honor

To honor is to highly esteem someone for their integrity, honesty, uprightness, or courage. We pay homage to our veterans for their service to our country; we laud athletes, students, entertainers, ministers, and others who achieve excellence in their fields. In other words, we honor people we value and deem worthy of our respect.

The following verses tell us to honor the Lord with our tithes, our adoration, and everything we have. Far above all others, God is worthy of *all* our honor and praise.

Father, praising You and rejoicing in You must be high on my priority list. Proclaiming Your love to others must never be lacking in my life. Thank You that I am able to rejoice in You! Amen.

Honor the LORD with your possessions,
and with the firstfruits of all your increase.
PROVERBS 3:9 NKJV

Children, obey your parents because you belong to the Lord,
for this is the right thing to do. "Honor your father and mother."
This is the first commandment with a promise: If you honor
your father and mother, "things will go well for you,
and you will have a long life on the earth."
EPHESIANS 6:1–3 NLT

She is more precious than jewels; and nothing you desire
compares with her. Long life is in her right hand;
in her left hand are riches and honor.
PROVERBS 3:15–16 NASB

Honour thy father and thy mother: that thy days may be
long upon the land which the LORD thy God giveth thee.
EXODUS 20:12 KJV

*Let our actions make us worthy of the blessing we have
received and [pray] that God will continue to bless us!*
DIANE ALBERS

Hope

*H*ave you ever hoped for something? Maybe a bigger house? A smaller dress size? A day to yourself? Or maybe more serious things like a physical healing or restoration of your marriage?

The word *hope* in the Greek translation is *elpis*, meaning "confident expectation in the unseen future" or "the happy expectation of good."

Hope launches a positive outlook. Without it, lives remain fragmented and broken, personal dreams go unrealized, and sick hearts lose the capacity to cope. Hope tells you to hold on in anticipation and expectation—because something good is just ahead!

Father God, the joy has gone out of my life. I need Your reassurance that You will never give me a burden without helping me bear it. Be my strong hope of a better future. Amen.

For I know the thoughts that I think toward you, says the LORD,
thoughts of peace and not of evil, to give you a future and a hope.

JEREMIAH 29:11 NKJV

Dear friends, we are already God's children, but he has not yet
shown us what we will be like when Christ appears. But we do
know that we will be like him, for we will see him as he
really is. And all who have this eager expectation
will keep themselves pure, just as he is pure.

1 JOHN 3:2–3 NLT

And not only so, but we glory in tribulations also: knowing
that tribulation worketh patience; and patience,
experience; and experience, hope:
and hope maketh not ashamed.

ROMANS 5:3–5 KJV

The hope of the righteous is gladness,
but the expectation of the wicked perishes.

PROVERBS 10:28 NASB

Praise be to the God and Father of our Lord Jesus Christ!
In his great mercy he has given us new birth into a living hope
through the resurrection of Jesus Christ from the dead.

1 PETER 1:3 NIV

*Lord, You are my hope in an often hopeless world. You are my hope
of heaven, my hope of peace, my hope of change, purpose,
and unconditional love. Fill the reservoir of my heart to
overflowing with the joy that real hope brings. Amen.*

"Blessed is the man who trusts in the Lord,
and whose hope is the Lord."
JEREMIAH 17:7 NKJV

"The Lord is my portion," says my soul, "Therefore I have hope
in Him." The Lord is good to those who wait for Him, to the
person who seeks Him. It is good that he waits
silently for the salvation of the Lord.
LAMENTATIONS 3:24–26 NASB

But since we belong to the day, let us be sober, putting on faith
and love as a breastplate, and the hope of salvation as a helmet.
1 THESSALONIANS 5:8 NIV

My soul faints for Your salvation, but I hope in Your word.
PSALM 119:81 NKJV

Instead, you must worship Christ as Lord of your
life. And if someone asks about your hope as
a believer, always be ready to explain it.
1 PETER 3:15 NLT

*When all hope seems lost, Lord, be with those who suffer. Help them to
never abandon hope, for all things are possible with You. Amen.*

In hope of eternal life, which God, that cannot lie,
promised before the world began.
TITUS 1:2 KJV

For we through the Spirit, by faith,
are waiting for the hope of righteousness.
GALATIANS 5:5 NASB

But Christ is faithful as the Son over God's house.
And we are his house, if indeed we hold firmly to
our confidence and the hope in which we glory.
HEBREWS 3:6 NIV

That by two immutable things, in which it is impossible for God
to lie, we might have strong consolation, who have fled for refuge
to lay hold of the hope set before us. This hope we have as an
anchor of the soul, both sure and steadfast, and which
enters the Presence behind the veil.
HEBREWS 6:18–19 NKJV

I pray that God, the source of hope, will fill you completely with
joy and peace because you trust in him. Then you will overflow
with confident hope through the power of the Holy Spirit.
ROMANS 15:13 NLT

*Lord, there is so much I do not understand about You. Still, I can see
the effects of Your actions, the evidence that You are still active
in my daily life. I do not need to physically see You to
believe. Your evidence is everywhere. Amen.*

To whom God would make known what is the riches of the
glory of this mystery among the Gentiles; which is
Christ in you, the hope of glory.
COLOSSIANS 1:27 KJV

Who through Him are believers in God, who raised Him from the
dead and gave Him glory, so that your faith and hope are in God.
1 PETER 1:21 NASB

"And I have the same hope in God as these men themselves
have, that there will be a resurrection of both
the righteous and the wicked."
ACTS 24:15 NIV

And we desire that each one of you show the same diligence
to the full assurance of hope until the end.
HEBREWS 6:11 NKJV

There is one body and one Spirit, just as also you
were called in one hope of your calling.
EPHESIANS 4:4 NASB

Lord, remind me every day that my hope is set on You.
That You are the author and finisher of my faith. Amen.

For in this hope we were saved. But hope that is seen is no hope
at all. Who hopes for what they already have? But if we hope
for what we do not yet have, we wait for it patiently.
ROMANS 8:24–25 NIV

LORD, I hope for Your salvation, and I do Your commandments.
PSALM 119:166 NKJV

Since this new way gives us such confidence, we can be very bold.
2 CORINTHIANS 3:12 NLT

The eyes of your understanding being enlightened; that ye may
know what is the hope of his calling, and what the riches
of the glory of his inheritance in the saints.
EPHESIANS 1:18 KJV

According to my earnest expectation and hope, that I will not
be put to shame in anything, but that with all boldness,
Christ will even now, as always, be exalted in my
body, whether by life or by death.
PHILIPPIANS 1:20 NASB

Looking for that blessed hope, and the glorious appearing
of the great God and our Saviour Jesus Christ.
TITUS 2:13 KJV

*Lord, I know that You are the one at work in me; Your Spirit is a part
of me, and You guide my thoughts and actions. Thank You for that.
I don't know what I would do if I had to live life on my own. Amen.*

Remember your word to your servant,
for you have given me hope.
Psalm 119:49 NIV

Why are you cast down, O my soul? And why are you
disquieted within me? Hope in God; for I shall yet praise
Him, the help of my countenance and my God.
Psalm 42:11 NKJV

Which come from your confident hope of what God has reserved
for you in heaven. You have had this expectation ever since
you first heard the truth of the Good News.
Colossians 1:5 NLT

Now faith is the assurance of things hoped for,
the conviction of things not seen.
Hebrews 11:1 NASB

But God will never forget the needy; the hope of
the afflicted will never perish.
Psalm 9:18 NIV

Optimism is the faith that leads to achievement.
Nothing can be done without hope and confidence.
Helen Keller

Hospitality

*W*omen and hospitality go together like coffee and cream. Generally, women are the ones who host family gatherings, church dinners, kids' birthday parties, and so much more.

Back in the 1930s and '40s, vagabonds would often go house-to-house for food. Without hesitation, the woman of the house would serve the stranger a hot meal. Of course, that kind of hospitality is dangerous today. Yet we should continue to open our homes and give to those we *do* know. After all, a hospitable woman not only opens her home, she opens her heart.

Lord, I want my house to be Your house—a house of prayer, a place of comfort and peace, a refuge to those in need. Help me make our home a blessing for all who pass through its door. Amen.

Do not forget to entertain strangers, for by so doing
some have unwittingly entertained angels.
HEBREWS 13:2 NKJV

"Do not take advantage of foreigners who live among you in your
land. Treat them like native-born Israelites, and love them as you
love yourself. Remember that you were once foreigners living
in the land of Egypt. I am the LORD your God."
LEVITICUS 19:33–34 NLT

Use hospitality one to another without grudging.
1 PETER 4:9 KJV

For the overseer must be above reproach as God's steward,
not self-willed, not quick-tempered, not addicted to wine,
not pugnacious, not fond of sordid gain, but hospitable,
loving what is good, sensible, just, devout, self-controlled.
TITUS 1:7–8 NASB

Distributing to the needs of the saints, given to hospitality.
ROMANS 12:13 NKJV

*Father God, it seems my cynical attitude is keeping me from
performing acts of hospitality. Please give me the faith and strength
to do what needs to be done, not because I want a reward
but because it is an honor to do Your work. Amen.*

"Instead, invite the poor, the crippled, the lame, and the blind.
Then at the resurrection of the righteous, God will reward
you for inviting those who could not repay you."
LUKE 14:13–14 NLT

Nor shall you glean your vineyard, nor shall you gather the fallen fruit of your vineyard; you shall leave them for the needy and for the stranger. I am the LORD your God.

LEVITICUS 19:10 NASB

Wisdom has built her house; she has set up its seven pillars. She has prepared her meat and mixed her wine; she has also set her table. She has sent out her servants, and she calls from the highest point of the city, "Let all who are simple come to my house!" To those who have no sense she says, "Come, eat my food and drink the wine I have mixed."

PROVERBS 9:1–5 NIV

Well reported of for good works; if she have brought up children, if she have lodged strangers, if she have washed the saints' feet, if she have relieved the afflicted, if she have diligently followed every good work.

1 TIMOTHY 5:10 KJV

Suppose a brother or sister is without clothes and daily food. If one of you says to them, "Go in peace; keep warm and well fed," but does nothing about their physical needs, what good is it?

JAMES 2:15–16 NIV

Father, be with us today and stay near as we strive to raise our family in a way that will please You and allow us to accomplish whatever You have planned. Use our home as a place to glorify You and reach out to others. Amen.

"He ensures that orphans and widows receive justice.
He shows love to the foreigners living among you
and gives them food and clothing."
DEUTERONOMY 10:18 NLT

"Then the King will say to those on His right hand, 'Come,
you blessed of My Father, inherit the kingdom prepared for you from
the foundation of the world: for I was hungry and you gave Me food;
I was thirsty and you gave Me drink; I was a stranger and you took
Me in; I was naked and you clothed Me; I was sick and you visited
Me; I was in prison and you came to Me.' . . . And the King will
answer and say to them, 'Assuredly, I say to you, inasmuch as you
did it to one of the least of these My brethren, you did it to Me.' "
MATTHEW 25:34–36, 40 NKJV

For whosoever shall give you a cup of water to
drink in my name, because ye belong to Christ,
verily I say unto you, he shall not lose his reward.
MARK 9:41 KJV

*Just allow your guest to feel at ease because you
are, whatever the state of your house. This is an
important element to being a gracious host.*
LINDA DAVIS ZUMBEHL

Humility

*N*ineteenth-century missionary Mary Slessor said: "Blessed is the man or woman who is able to serve cheerfully in the second rank—a big test."

Serving in the limelight is one thing, but serving absent of accolades and applause is another. Those who take a backseat and work as hard as if they were in the front seat are diligent. But those who take a backseat and have no thought of taking credit for their deeds are humble.

Jesus said, "The first shall be last and the last shall be first" in God's kingdom. Humility leads to greatness, and great people are the ones who are humble.

Father, I need a reminder that what I should be is a servant. I get so wrapped up in the need to maintain order that I forget my job—to meet the needs of others. Please give me a servant's heart. Amen.

Be of the same mind toward one another; do not be haughty
in mind, but associate with the lowly. Do not be
wise in your own estimation.
ROMANS 12:16 NASB

This is what the LORD says: "Let not the wise boast of their
wisdom or the strong boast of their strength
or the rich boast of their riches."
JEREMIAH 9:23 NIV

If I must boast, I will boast in the things
which concern my infirmity.
2 CORINTHIANS 11:30 NKJV

Don't brag about tomorrow, since you don't
know what the day will bring.
PROVERBS 27:1 NLT

Whosoever therefore shall humble himself as this little child,
the same is greatest in the kingdom of heaven.
MATTHEW 18:4 KJV

*Vows to You must be kept, Father. You not only remember Your
promises to us, You never forget our promises to You. Help me
treat my vows to You seriously, Lord. If sacrifices are
required of me, let me bear them in faith. Amen.*

"When you are cast down, you will speak with confidence,
and the humble person He will save."
JOB 22:29 NASB

In the same way, you who are younger, submit yourselves to your
elders. All of you, clothe yourselves with humility toward one
another, because, "God opposes the proud but shows favor to
the humble." Humble yourselves, therefore, under God's
mighty hand, that he may lift you up in due time.
1 PETER 5:5–6 NIV

The LORD mocks the mockers but is gracious to the humble.
PROVERBS 3:34 NLT

"Blessed are the poor in spirit, for theirs is the kingdom of heaven."
MATTHEW 5:3 NASB

"Listen to me, you who pursue righteousness and who seek the
LORD: Look to the rock from which you were cut and
to the quarry from which you were hewn."
ISAIAH 51:1 NIV

*Lord, thank You for asking Jesus to pay the high price for what I've
done. The thought of His sacrifice and Your unending grace
humbles me beyond words. "Thank You" will never be enough. Amen.*

LORD, You have heard the desire of the humble; You will prepare
their heart; You will cause Your ear to hear.
PSALM 10:17 NKJV

Lord, my heart is not haughty, nor mine eyes lofty:
neither do I exercise myself in great matters,
or in things too high for me.
PSALM 131:1 KJV

And whosoever shall exalt himself shall be abased;
and he that shall humble himself shall be exalted.
MATTHEW 23:12 KJV

Pride leads to disgrace, but with humility comes wisdom.
PROVERBS 11:2 NLT

For though the LORD is exalted, yet He regards the lowly,
but the haughty He knows from afar.
PSALM 138:6 NASB

*Lord, as a mother, I need to take advantage of the teachable moments
You give me to teach my children the truths about Your Word. I pray
that with Your help, I'll never let an opportunity pass by. Amen.*

But made Himself of no reputation, taking the form of a
bondservant, and coming in the likeness of men. And being found
in appearance as a man, He humbled Himself and became obedient
to the point of death, even the death of the cross. Therefore God
also has highly exalted Him and given Him the
name which is above every name.

PHILIPPIANS 2:7–9 NKJV

Humble yourselves in the presence of the Lord,
and He will exalt you.

JAMES 4:10 NASB

For this is what the high and exalted One says—he who lives
forever, whose name is holy: "I live in a high and holy place, but
also with the one who is contrite and lowly in spirit, to revive
the spirit of the lowly and to revive the heart of the contrite."

ISAIAH 57:15 NIV

When he maketh inquisition for blood, he remembereth
them: he forgetteth not the cry of the humble.

PSALM 9:12 KJV

*All of the charm and beauty a woman may have amounts to nothing
if her ambitions are self-centered. But if she reflects her Creator
and assumes the posture of a graceful servant, she cannot
help but command high respect and love.*

JEANNE HENDRICKS

Joy

*D*o you know someone who has a spirit of joy? No matter what happens in life, she always has an uplifting word and a glowing smile. She sparkles with joy brighter than polished diamonds and, not surprisingly, everyone enjoys her company.

The scriptures encourage us to delight in the Lord that way—to illuminate with joy about our salvation and the goodness of God. Our joy should shine in such a way that it lights the pathway to lead others to Christ.

One day, we will rejoice in heaven. That fact alone should cause us to jump for joy!

There's no mistaking, Lord. You've made it clear that I'm to be joyful in each and every task. The next time I'm tempted to complain about the mounds of work, remind me to turn the murmuring into praise. Amen.

But the angel reassured them. "Don't be afraid!" he said.
"I bring you good news that will bring great joy to all people."
LUKE 2:10 NLT

The LORD is my strength and my shield; my heart trusted
in him, and I am helped: therefore my heart greatly
rejoiceth; and with my song will I praise him.
PSALM 28:7 KJV

Rejoice in the Lord always; again I will say, rejoice!
PHILIPPIANS 4:4 NASB

"Until now you have not asked for anything in my name.
Ask and you will receive, and your joy will be complete."
JOHN 16:24 NIV

Be glad in the LORD and rejoice, you righteous;
and shout for joy, all you upright in heart!
PSALM 32:11 NKJV

*Jesus. What a wonderful name! It is the only name we need to call
upon for salvation. I praise You for being the Way,
the Truth, and the Life, Lord. Amen.*

Evil people are trapped by sin, but the righteous
escape, shouting for joy.
PROVERBS 29:6 NLT

As sorrowful, yet always rejoicing; as poor, yet making many
rich; as having nothing, and yet possessing all things.
2 CORINTHIANS 6:10 KJV

So the ransomed of the LORD shall return, and come to Zion with
singing, with everlasting joy on their heads. They shall obtain
joy and gladness; sorrow and sighing shall flee away.
ISAIAH 51:11 NKJV

"The master was full of praise. 'Well done, my good
and faithful servant. You have been faithful in handling
this small amount, so now I will give you many
more responsibilities. Let's celebrate together!' "
MATTHEW 25:21 NLT

Rejoice ye in that day, and leap for joy: for, behold,
your reward is great in heaven: for in the like
manner did their fathers unto the prophets.
LUKE 6:23 KJV

*I am not worthy of Your gifts of mercy and forgiveness,
Father, but I accept them with joy. Amen.*

Shout joyfully to the LORD, all the earth. Serve the LORD
with gladness; come before Him with joyful singing.
PSALM 100:1–2 NASB

"I am coming to you now, but I say these things while I am
still in the world, so that they may have the full
measure of my joy within them."
JOHN 17:13 NIV

All the days of the afflicted are evil, but he who
is of a merry heart has a continual feast.
PROVERBS 15:15 NKJV

Not that we lord it over your faith, but are workers with you
for your joy; for in your faith you are standing firm.
2 CORINTHIANS 1:24 NASB

Is anyone among you in trouble? Let them pray. Is anyone
happy? Let them sing songs of praise.
JAMES 5:13 NIV

*Father, fill our hearts full of You and Your Word; then we can sing
with grace and joy. My family and I can proclaim Your goodness
to all those we meet. What a blessing! Amen.*

For our heart shall rejoice in Him, because we have
trusted in His holy name.
PSALM 33:21 NKJV

Singing psalms and hymns and spiritual songs among
yourselves, and making music to the Lord in your hearts.
EPHESIANS 5:19 NLT

Laughter lightens the load.
PATSY CLAIRMONT

Kindness

*Y*ears ago, Oprah Winfrey encouraged her audience to engage in "random acts of kindness." She led the crusade through personal example with deeds such as paying the toll for the person in the vehicle behind her. Her message was simple: extend one act of kindness to a stranger each day.

Kindness is rooted in a giving heart. The virtue is displayed in small ways like driving an elderly patient to the doctor, cooking a meal for a shut-in, babysitting for a busy mom, or simply sharing a smile.

When kindness is the rule, there's nothing random about it.

Lord, You welcomed me into Your family with love and acceptance.
Help me be as kind to others as You have been to me—
cheerfully welcoming everyone. Amen.

"Give to everyone who asks of you, and whoever takes
away what is yours, do not demand it back."
LUKE 6:30 NASB

Do not repay evil with evil or insult with insult. On the contrary,
repay evil with blessing, because to this you were
called so that you may inherit a blessing.
1 PETER 3:9 NIV

She opens her mouth with wisdom, and on her
tongue is the law of kindness.
PROVERBS 31:26 NKJV

Since God chose you to be the holy people he loves,
you must clothe yourselves with tenderhearted mercy,
kindness, humility, gentleness, and patience.
COLOSSIANS 3:12 NLT

And to godliness brotherly kindness; and to brotherly kindness
charity. For if these things be in you, and abound. . .ye shall neither
be barren nor unfruitful in the knowledge of our Lord Jesus Christ.
2 PETER 1:7–8 KJV

*Lord, may I never hesitate to forgive anyone
when You have already forgiven me. Amen.*

Each of us is to please his neighbor
for his good, to his edification.
ROMANS 15:2 NASB

As we have therefore opportunity, let us do good unto all men,
especially unto them who are of the household of faith.
GALATIANS 6:10 KJV

"This is what the LORD Almighty said: 'Administer true justice;
show mercy and compassion to one another. Do not oppress
the widow or the fatherless, the foreigner or the poor.
Do not plot evil against each other.' "
ZECHARIAH 7:9–10 NIV

But in everything commending ourselves as servants of God,
in much endurance, in afflictions, in hardships, in distresses. . .
in purity, in knowledge, in patience, in kindness, in the Holy Spirit,
in genuine love. . .as sorrowful yet always rejoicing, as poor yet
making many rich, as having nothing yet possessing all things.
2 CORINTHIANS 6:4, 6, 10 NASB

Be happy with those who are happy,
and weep with those who weep.
· ROMANS 12:15 NLT

*True love is kind, not prideful or self-seeking. Lord, fill me with
compassion for my fellow Christians so I might be a godly example
of love and understanding. I want to emulate You, Jesus. Amen.*

He who despises his neighbor sins,
but happy is he who is gracious to the poor.
PROVERBS 14:21 NASB

"Give to the one who asks you, and do not turn away
from the one who wants to borrow from you."
MATTHEW 5:42 NIV

He can have compassion on those who are ignorant and
going astray, since he himself is also subject to weakness.
HEBREWS 5:2 NKJV

The desire of a man is his kindness: and a poor man is
better than a liar. The fear of the LORD tendeth to
life: and he that hath it shall abide satisfied.
PROVERBS 19:22–23 KJV

"The LORD bless you, my daughter!" Boaz exclaimed. "You are
showing even more family loyalty now than you did before, for you
have not gone after a younger man, whether rich or poor. Now don't
worry about a thing, my daughter. I will do what is necessary,
for everyone in town knows you are a virtuous woman."
RUTH 3:10–11 NLT

*Let no one ever come to you without leaving better and happier.
Be the living expression of God's kindness: kindness in your
face, kindness in your eyes, kindness in your smile.*
MOTHER TERESA

Love of God

Do you love God? Some would think that a trick question. Of course every Christian loves God! Don't they?

The following scriptures address this subject. They tell us that if we love God, we will—among other things—seek Him and keep His commandments. Placing God first and desiring His will above our own demonstrates our love and devotion to the One who has done, and continues to do, so much for us.

Loving God is more than lip service, it's God-service.

Lord, I really want to grow spiritually. I need to—for my own daily walk with You and, most importantly, because You've commanded me to. Thank You for giving me the strength to fulfill your commands and to grow spiritually. Amen.

The LORD watches over all who love him,
but all the wicked he will destroy.
PSALM 145:20 NIV

"Therefore take careful heed to yourselves,
that you love the LORD your God."
JOSHUA 23:11 NKJV

"Understand, therefore, that the LORD your God is indeed God.
He is the faithful God who keeps his covenant for a thousand
generations and lavishes his unfailing love on those
who love him and obey his commands."
DEUTERONOMY 7:9 NLT

And Jesus answered him, The first of all the commandments is,
Hear, O Israel; The Lord our God is one Lord: And thou shalt
love the Lord thy God with all thy heart, and with all thy soul,
and with all thy mind, and with all thy strength: this is the
first commandment. And the second is like, namely this,
Thou shalt love thy neighbour as thyself. There is
none other commandment greater than these.
MARK 12:29–31 KJV

That Christ may dwell in your hearts through faith; that you,
being rooted and grounded in love, may be able to comprehend
with all the saints what is the width and length and depth and
height—to know the love of Christ which passes knowledge;
that you may be filled with all the fullness of God.
EPHESIANS 3:17–19 NKJV

Lord, I pray that my children and their children and each
successive generation will understand that all the glory
for our many blessings belongs to You. Without You
we would be nothing and would have nothing. Amen.

Jesus told them, "If God were your Father, you would love
me, because I have comes to you from God. I am
not here on my own, but he sent me."
JOHN 8:42 NLT

Thank You for the work You have given me, Father, with its
opportunities to be of service to others and to You. You have made
me a woman of value, and my contribution is great. Amen.

"You shall love the LORD your God with all your heart
and with all your soul and with all your might."
DEUTERONOMY 6:5 NASB

Do not love the world or anything in the world. If anyone
loves the world, love for the Father is not in them.
1 JOHN 2:15 NIV

"I love those who love me, and those who seek
me diligently will find me."
PROVERBS 8:17 NKJV

I will declare Your name to My brethren; in the
midst of the assembly I will praise You.
PSALM 22:22 NKJV

For God is not unrighteous to forget your work and labour of love, which ye have shewed toward his name.
HEBREWS 6:10 KJV

Take delight in the LORD, and he will give you your heart's desires.
PSALM 37:4 NLT

And we know that all things work together for good to them that love God, to them who are the called according to his purpose.
ROMANS 8:28 KJV

And await the mercy of our Lord Jesus Christ, who will bring you eternal life. In this way, you will keep yourselves safe in God's love.
JUDE 21 NLT

And we have known and believed the love that God hath to us. God is love; and he that dwelleth in love dwelleth in God, and God in him. Herein is our love made perfect, that we may have boldness in the day of judgment: because as he is, so are we in this world. There is no fear in love; but perfect love casteth out fear: because fear hath torment. He that feareth is not made perfect in love. We love him, because he first loved us.
1 JOHN 4:16–19 KJV

"He who has My commandments and keeps them is the one who loves Me; and he who loves Me will be loved by My Father, and I will love him and will disclose Myself to him."
JOHN 14:21 NASB

The greatest need in the world today is love. . .
More love for each other and more love for God above!
HELEN STEINER RICE

Love for Others

*G*od commands us to love others, and guess what? That includes our enemies too.

It's easy to love those who love us or—at the very least—to love those who are somewhat lovable. But our enemies?

Enemy is a strong word, but you get the picture. It describes anyone who is hostile or adversarial toward you. Like the coworker who diminishes your job position while aggrandizing hers. Or the neighbor who persistently gossips about you despite your efforts to help her.

God's love compels us to love, forgive, understand, and pray for one another. . .even the unlovable.

Lord, help me not to be quick to judge or oppose love between others.
Let me give love time to do its work. I may never see the result
I want, but I am sure it is in Your hands. Amen.

Be devoted to one another in love.
Honor one another above yourselves.
ROMANS 12:10 NIV

But concerning brotherly love you have no need that I should write
to you, for you yourselves are taught by God to love one another.
1 THESSALONIANS 4:9 NKJV

For the whole law can be summed up in this one
command: "Love your neighbor as yourself."
GALATIANS 5:14 NLT

Beloved, if God so loved us, we also ought to love one another.
No one has seen God at any time; if we love one another,
God abides in us, and His love is perfected in us.
1 JOHN 4:11–12 NASB

*Lord, thank You for Your attention to those who struggle, for Your
provision, and for the promise that their dreams will eventually come
true. I wish them the contentment I am now enjoying. Amen.*

And now these three remain: faith, hope and love.
But the greatest of these is love.
1 CORINTHIANS 13:13 NIV

Thou shalt not avenge, nor bear any grudge against the
children of thy people, but thou shalt love thy
neighbour as thyself: I am the LORD.
LEVITICUS 19:18 KJV

Leave there thy gift before the altar, and go thy way; first be reconciled to thy brother, and then come and offer thy gift.

MATTHEW 5:24 KJV

If I speak with the tongues of men and of angels, but do not have love, I have become a noisy gong or a clanging cymbal. If I have the gift of prophecy, and know all mysteries and all knowledge; and if I have all faith, so as to remove mountains, but do not have love, I am nothing. And if I give all my possessions to feed the poor, and if I surrender my body to be burned, but do not have love, it profits me nothing.

1 CORINTHIANS 13:1–3 NASB

Let no debt remain outstanding, except the continuing debt to love one another, for whoever loves others has fulfilled the law.

ROMANS 13:8 NIV

And to godliness brotherly kindness;
and to brotherly kindness charity.

2 PETER 1:7 KJV

And because of your knowledge shall the weak brother perish, for whom Christ died? But when you thus sin against the brethren, and wound their weak conscience, you sin against Christ.

1 CORINTHIANS 8:11–12 NKJV

Thank You, Lord, for putting other godly moms in my life. They face many temptations that I face, but they've committed themselves to purity, so together we can encourage one another. What a blessing! Amen.

Let us think of ways to motivate one
another to acts of love and good works.
HEBREWS 10:24 NLT

In this the children of God are manifest, and the children of the
devil: whosoever doeth not righteousness is not of God,
neither he that loveth not his brother.
1 JOHN 3:10 KJV

If someone says, "I love God," but hates a fellow believer,
that person is a liar; for if we don't love people we can see,
how can we love God, whom we cannot see? And he
has given us this command: Those who love God
must also love their fellow believers.
1 JOHN 4:20–21 NLT

Since you have in obedience to the truth purified your souls
for a sincere love of the brethren, fervently love
one another from the heart.
1 PETER 1:22 NASB

I say this to your shame. Is it so, that there is not a wise man among
you, not even one, who will be able to judge between his brethren?
But brother goes to law against brother, and that before unbelievers!
Now therefore, it is already an utter failure for you that you go to
law against one another. Why do you not rather accept wrong?
Why do you not rather let yourselves be cheated? No,
you yourselves do wrong and cheat, and you
do these things to your brethren!
1 CORINTHIANS 6:5–8 NKJV

Lord, help me to show compassion for my children and also for strangers. You were the best example. You loved everyone, Lord. Help me do the same and in doing so set an example for my children. Amen.

"A new commandment I give to you, that you love one another, even as I have loved you, that you also love one another. By this all men will know that you are My disciples, if you have love for one another."
JOHN 13:34–35 NASB

Dear friends, let us love one another, for love comes from God. Everyone who loves has been born of God and knows God. Whoever does not love does not know God, because God is love. This is how God showed his love among us: He sent his one and only Son into the world that we might live through him. This is love: not that we loved God, but that he loved us and sent his Son as an atoning sacrifice for our sins. Dear friends, since God so loved us, we also ought to love one another.
1 JOHN 4:7–11 NIV

Finally, all of you be of one mind, having compassion for one another; love as brothers, be tenderhearted, be courteous.
1 PETER 3:8 NKJV

If I put my own good name before the other's highest good, then I know nothing of Calvary love.
AMY CARMICHAEL

Meekness

*H*ow can a Type-A lady with an exuberant, take-charge, outgoing personality, exhibit meekness? Wouldn't that contradict who she really is?

Jesus not only encourages meekness in His beatitudes, He described Himself as "meek and lowly in heart" (Matthew 11:29 KJV). Yet Jesus was no pushover.

Meekness isn't our outward behavior, but an inwrought grace of the soul. It is a tempered spirit fully surrendered to God, one that accepts His dealings without dispute or resistance. Meekness demonstrates full devotion to and humility before God.

Jesus said that the meek will inherit the earth. And that includes Type-A personalities too.

Thank You for the times I am humbled, Lord. You are always here—
to listen, to forgive, and to heal. Lord, help me to be repentant,
to be willing to be brought low. Heal me, Lord. Amen.

The poor will eat and be satisfied. All who seek the LORD will
praise him. Their hearts will rejoice with everlasting joy.
PSALM 22:26 NLT

Great is our Lord, and of great power: his understanding is
infinite. The LORD lifteth up the meek: he casteth
the wicked down to the ground.
PSALM 147:5–6 KJV

The afflicted also will increase their gladness in the LORD,
and the needy of mankind will rejoice in the Holy One of Israel.
ISAIAH 29:19 NASB

Wives, in the same way submit yourselves to your own husbands
so that, if any of them do not believe the word, they may be won
over without words by the behavior of their wives. . . . Your beauty
should not come from outward adornment, such as elaborate
hairstyles and the wearing of gold jewelry or fine clothes.
Rather, it should be that of your inner self, the unfading
beauty of a gentle and quiet spirit, which is
of great worth in God's sight.
1 PETER 3:1, 3–4 NIV

Seek the LORD, all you meek of the earth, who have upheld His
justice. Seek righteousness, seek humility. It may be that
you will be hidden in the day of the LORD's anger.
ZEPHANIAH 2:3 NKJV

*I want my life to be a sacrifice for You, Lord. Help me live a life
of praise for You before my children. Guide me in showing my
children how to make the sacrifice of praise to You. Amen.*

Take my yoke upon you, and learn of me; for I am meek
and lowly in heart: and ye shall find rest unto your souls.
MATTHEW 11:29 KJV

"Blessed are the gentle, for they shall inherit the earth."
MATTHEW 5:5 NASB

Good and upright is the LORD; therefore he instructs sinners
in his ways. He guides the humble in what is
right and teaches them his way.
PSALM 25:8–9 NIV

Brethren, if a man is overtaken in any trespass, you who
are spiritual restore such a one in a spirit of gentleness,
considering yourself lest you also be tempted. Bear one
another's burdens, and so fulfill the law of Christ.
GALATIANS 6:1–2 NKJV

For the LORD delights in his people;
he crowns the humble with victory.
PSALM 149:4 NLT

We can do no great things; only small things with great love.
MOTHER TERESA

Mercy

God is merciful. If He weren't, most of us would be in big trouble! The Greek translation of *mercy* means "an outward manifestation of pity; it assumes need on the part of him who receives it, and the resources adequate to meet the need on the part of him who shows it."

If we love when wronged, we show mercy. If we give or forgive despite our grievances, we exhibit mercy. And if we understand those who are misunderstood, we are merciful.

Teamed with goodness, mercy shall follow believers all the days of their lives (Psalm 23:6). Lord, have mercy!

Lord, I don't know if I'll ever understand why You sacrificed Yourself for me. But, from the depths of my being, I want to shout praises to You and also tell the whole world what You did for all of us. Amen.

Be ye therefore merciful, as your Father also is merciful.
LUKE 6:36 KJV

But You, O Lord, are a God merciful and gracious,
slow to anger and abundant in lovingkindness and truth.
PSALM 86:15 NASB

But you must return to your God; maintain love
and justice, and wait for your God always.
HOSEA 12:6 NIV

"Blessed are the merciful, for they shall obtain mercy."
MATTHEW 5:7 NKJV

We give great honor to those who endure under suffering.
For instance, you know about Job, a man of great endurance.
You can see how the Lord was kind to him at the end,
for the Lord is full of tenderness and mercy.
JAMES 5:11 NLT

Heavenly Father, help me show my children the way to You while they are so eager to learn. I want to teach them about Your grace and mercy—the wonderful gifts You've made available to everyone. Amen.

For thou, Lord, art good, and ready to forgive; and plenteous
in mercy unto all them that call upon thee.
PSALM 86:5 KJV

He has told you, O man, what is good; and what does the
LORD require of you but to do justice, to love kindness,
and to walk humbly with your God?
MICAH 6:8 NASB

For God has imprisoned everyone in disobedience
so he could have mercy on everyone.
ROMANS 11:32 NLT

The LORD is good to all: and his tender
mercies are over all his works.
PSALM 145:9 KJV

Do not let kindness and truth leave you; bind them around your
neck, write them on the tablet of your heart. So you will find
favor and good repute in the sight of God and man.
PROVERBS 3:3–4 NASB

*Lord, may those I work with always see You in my life
and be brought closer to You though me. Amen.*

Whoever conceals their sins does not prosper, but the one
who confesses and renounces them finds mercy.
PROVERBS 28:13 NIV

But God, who is rich in mercy, because of His great love with which
He loved us, even when we were dead in trespasses, made us alive
together with Christ (by grace you have been saved).
EPHESIANS 2:4–5 NKJV

He saved us, not because of the righteous things we had done,
but because of his mercy. He washed away our sins, giving us a
new birth and new life through the Holy Spirit. He generously
poured out the Spirit upon us through Jesus Christ our Savior.
Because of his grace he made us right in his sight and
gave us confidence that we will inherit eternal life.
TITUS 3:5–7 NLT

Let the wicked forsake his way, and the unrighteous man his
thoughts: and let him return unto the LORD, and he will have
mercy upon him; and to our God, for he will abundantly pardon.
ISAIAH 55:7 KJV

Mercy and truth have met together;
righteousness and peace have kissed.
PSALM 85:10 NKJV

"For I will be merciful to their iniquities, and I will remember their sins no more." When He said, "A new covenant," He has made the first obsolete. But whatever is becoming obsolete and growing old is ready to disappear.
Hebrews 8:12–13 nasb

Father, help me remember that my priorities are not necessarily the priorities of those I love, so please give me the sense to step back and allow everyone a little leeway to lead their own lives. Help me be supportive, not bossy. Amen.

"His mercy extends to those who fear him, from generation to generation."
Luke 1:50 niv

Surely goodness and mercy shall follow me all the days of my life: and I will dwell in the house of the Lord for ever.
Psalm 23:6 kjv

God deals with us from a merciful posture; His arms are open, His words are healing, He wants sinners to return to Him.
Martie Stowell

Modesty

*W*hat is true modesty? Current fashions often expose too much skin or fit too tightly, but God's Word tells every woman to dress appropriately. What we wear and how we wear it matters to God because it reflects our inner character and spirit.

Modesty, however, goes far beyond the superficial. A modest spirit is clothed in humility and holiness. A woman who exhibits modesty is not boastful—rather, she seasons her words with kindness and grace. Doing otherwise brings her more embarrassment than wearing her pajamas in public!

Heavenly Father, we live in a world that lifts up proud people.
Make us all aware of how much You value sacrifice. Help us to
have the humble spirit we need when we come before You. Amen.

And I want women to be modest in their appearance. They should wear decent and appropriate clothing and not draw attention to themselves by the way they fix their hair or by wearing gold or pearls or expensive clothes. For women who claim to be devoted to God should make themselves attractive by the good things they do.
1 TIMOTHY 2:9–10 NLT

Let no man deceive himself. If any man among you seemeth to be wise in this world, let him become a fool, that he may be wise.
1 CORINTHIANS 3:18 KJV

A man's pride will bring him low,
but a humble spirit will obtain honor.
PROVERBS 29:23 NASB

A woman with a gentle and quiet spirit is not only precious to God, but she is attractive to others also. She dresses appropriately, but it is her inner adornment that is noted because she is secure and at rest within her spirit.
CYNTHIA HEALD

Obedience

*E*lisabeth Elliot, wife of martyred missionary Jim Elliot, said, "God is God. Because He is God, He is worthy of my trust and obedience."

A successful Christian walk is based on our obedience to Christ. In fact, to obey God is to love, serve, trust, and believe Him.

Consider how it pleases you when your child obeys you without question or resistance. He or she simply trusts you at your word and does what you ask. Nice, huh? The same is true of our heavenly Father. It pleases Him when we trust Him enough to obey.

When Your purpose is revealed to me, Father, help me to accept my responsibility and do Your will. Amen.

"Now then, if you will indeed obey My voice and keep My
covenant, then you shall be My own possession among
all the peoples, for all the earth is Mine."
EXODUS 19:5 NASB

Be careful to obey all these regulations I am giving you, so that
it may always go well with you and your children after you,
because you will be doing what is good and right in
the eyes of the LORD your God.
DEUTERONOMY 12:28 NIV

"You shall therefore keep His statutes and His commandments which
I command you today, that it may go well with you and with your
children after you, and that you may prolong your days in the
land which the LORD your God is giving you for all time."
DEUTERONOMY 4:40 NKJV

My child, never forget the things I have taught you. Store my
commands in your heart. If you do this, you will live
many years, and your life will be satisfying.
PROVERBS 3:1–2 NLT

But whoso looketh into the perfect law of liberty, and continueth
therein, he being not a forgetful hearer, but a doer of
the work, this man shall be blessed in his deed.
JAMES 1:25 KJV

*Father, I admit that once in a while I have a temper tantrum,
disputing Your guidance and wanting my own way, but You have
never been wrong. Thank You for Your love and patience,
for I will always need Your guidance. Amen.*

The things you have learned and received and heard and seen in me, practice these things, and the God of peace will be with you.
PHILIPPIANS 4:9 NASB

"If they obey and serve him, they will spend the rest of their days in prosperity and their years in contentment."
JOB 36:11 NIV

"Not everyone who calls out to me, 'Lord! Lord!' will enter the Kingdom of Heaven. Only those who actually do the will of my Father in heaven will enter."
MATTHEW 7:21 NLT

"If you keep My commandments, you will abide in My love; just as I have kept My Father's commandments and abide in His love."
JOHN 15:10 NASB

"In that I command you today to love the LORD your God, to walk in His ways, and to keep His commandments, His statutes, and His judgments, that you may live and multiply; and the LORD your God will bless you in the land which you go to possess."
DEUTERONOMY 30:16 NKJV

Let us hear the conclusion of the whole matter: Fear God, and keep his commandments: for this is the whole duty of man.
ECCLESIASTES 12:13 KJV

Father, I want my children to know what I expect of them and then obey. Give me guidance to establish the right reward and discipline system. I need strength in that area, Lord. Amen.

"So if you ignore the least commandment and teach others to do the same, you will be called the least in the Kingdom of Heaven. But anyone who obeys God's laws and teaches them will be called great in the Kingdom of Heaven."
MATTHEW 5:19 NLT

For not the hearers of the law are just before God,
but the doers of the law shall be justified.
ROMANS 2:13 KJV

The world is passing away, and also its lusts;
but the one who does the will of God lives forever.
1 JOHN 2:17 NASB

He replied, "Blessed rather are those who hear
the word of God and obey it."
LUKE 11:28 NIV

"If you are willing and obedient,
you will eat the good things of the land."
ISAIAH 1:19 NIV

*Lord, I want to obey You in everything and also lead my family
to obey You. Through our obedience to You, help us to
reach many people for Your kingdom. Amen.*

"Therefore keep the words of this covenant, and do them,
that you may prosper in all that you do."
DEUTERONOMY 29:9 NKJV

Blessed are they that keep his testimonies,
and that seek him with the whole heart.
PSALM 119:2 KJV

Since we respected our earthly fathers who disciplined us,
shouldn't we submit even more to the discipline of
the Father of our spirits, and live forever?
HEBREWS 12:9 NLT

So then, my beloved, just as you have always obeyed, not as in
my presence only, but now much more in my absence,
work out your salvation with fear and trembling.
PHILIPPIANS 2:12 NASB

*The only way I will keep a pliable, obedient spirit in the larger
decisions is to look to Him and to obey in the smaller ones.*
CATHERINE MARSHALL

Patience

*P*atience is a lost virtue in our fast-paced, I-want-it-now society. We want results and we want them immediately! Just ask any woman on a diet. After a week or so, some of us fall off the wagon when the number on the scale doesn't drop quickly enough.

Our impatience surfaces in other ways too—everything from waiting in a store checkout line to waiting for answered prayer.

Attaining patience is a process, often birthed from endurance on the battlefield of trials. Yet patience is a virtue worth working—and waiting—for.

Put a new song in my mouth, Lord. Let others see me being patient and waiting on You, no matter what difficulty I'm facing. Help them learn the same song of joy that You are giving me. Amen.

And a servant of the Lord must not quarrel but
be gentle to all, able to teach, patient.
2 TIMOTHY 2:24 NKJV

Be still in the presence of the LORD, and wait patiently for him to
act. Don't worry about evil people who prosper or fret about their
wicked schemes. Stop being angry! Turn from your rage! Do not
lose your temper—it only leads to harm. For the wicked will be
destroyed, but those who trust in the LORD will possess the land.
PSALM 37:7–9 NLT

For ye have need of patience, that, after ye have done
the will of God, ye might receive the promise.
HEBREWS 10:36 KJV

Here is the perseverance of the saints who keep the
commandments of God and their faith in Jesus.
REVELATION 14:12 NASB

Because you know that the testing of your faith produces
perseverance. Let perseverance finish its work so that
you may be mature and complete, not lacking anything.
JAMES 1:3–4 NIV

*Lord, I want to learn to be patient and trust in You.
I know that You will hear my cries and I will be
blessed. Thank You for this blessing. Amen.*

"But the ones that fell on the good ground are those who, having heard the word with a noble and good heart, keep it and bear fruit with patience."

LUKE 8:15 NKJV

In your patience possess ye your souls.

LUKE 21:19 KJV

For whatever things were written before were written for our learning, that we through the patience and comfort of the Scriptures might have hope. Now may the God of patience and comfort grant you to be like-minded toward one another, according to Christ Jesus.

ROMANS 15:4–5 NKJV

May the Lord lead your hearts into a full understanding and expression of the love of God and the patient endurance that comes from Christ.

2 THESSALONIANS 3:5 NLT

Therefore be patient, brethren, until the coming of the Lord. The farmer waits for the precious produce of the soil, being patient about it, until it gets the early and late rains. You too be patient; strengthen your hearts, for the coming of the Lord is near.

JAMES 5:7–8 NASB

Renew me. Give me the ability I need to be patient, no matter what trouble is around me. Let my joyful hope and faithful prayers build up my patience. Amen.

155

Therefore, since we are surrounded by such a great cloud of witnesses, let us throw off everything that hinders and the sin that so easily entangles. And let us run with perseverance the race marked out for us.

HEBREWS 12:1 NIV

That you do not become sluggish, but imitate those who through faith and patience inherit the promises.

HEBREWS 6:12 NKJV

Of course, you get no credit for being patient if you are beaten for doing wrong. But if you suffer for doing good and endure it patiently, God is pleased with you.

1 PETER 2:20 NLT

Better is the end of a thing than the beginning thereof: and the patient in spirit is better than the proud in spirit. Be not hasty in thy spirit to be angry: for anger resteth in the bosom of fools.

ECCLESIASTES 7:8–9 KJV

And so, having patiently waited, he obtained the promise.

HEBREWS 6:15 NASB

To those who by persistence in doing good seek glory, honor and immortality, he will give eternal life.

ROMANS 2:7 NIV

Obedience is the fruit of faith; patience, the bloom on the fruit.

CHRISTINA ROSSETTI

Peace

*H*ow do you describe peace? A day spent at the beach? An afternoon without phone calls and to-do lists? How about a stress-free week? Those things may initiate peace, but they are rarely the source of it.

God gives us a peace that surpasses human understanding—the kind of peace that prevails in the most difficult situations or alarming circumstances. Only the Lord can administer tranquility in the midst of life's storms.

Need peace? Relax and bask in the peace that only God provides.

Father, give me Your peace and an understanding that all things work together for good when I follow Your will. Amen.

"For the mountains shall depart and the hills be removed,
but My kindness shall not depart from you, nor shall My
covenant of peace be removed," says the LORD, who has
mercy on you. . . . "All your children shall be taught by the
LORD, and great shall be the peace of your children."
ISAIAH 54:10, 13 NKJV

I pray that God, the source of hope, will fill you completely with
joy and peace because you trust in him. Then you will overflow
with confident hope through the power of the Holy Spirit.
ROMANS 15:13 NLT

The LORD will give strength unto his people;
the LORD will bless his people with peace.
PSALM 29:11 KJV

When a man's ways are pleasing to the LORD,
he makes even his enemies to be at peace with him.
PROVERBS 16:7 NASB

"Blessed are the peacemakers,
for they will be called children of God."
MATTHEW 5:9 NIV

*Lord, help untangle my emotions and sort my jumbled thoughts.
Calm my restless spirit. Help me experience Your supernatural
peace in a real and tangible way. Amen.*

Deceit is in the heart of those who devise evil,
but counselors of peace have joy.
PROVERBS 12:20 NKJV

And those who are peacemakers will plant seeds of
peace and reap a harvest of righteousness.
JAMES 3:18 NLT

Do all that you can to live in peace with everyone.
ROMANS 12:18 NLT

And He will judge between the nations, and will render decisions
for many peoples; and they will hammer their swords into plow-
shares and their spears into pruning hooks. Nation will not lift up
sword against nation, and never again will they learn war.
ISAIAH 2:4 NASB

And the peace of God, which passeth all understanding,
shall keep your hearts and minds through Christ Jesus.
PHILIPPIANS 4:7 KJV

*Heavenly Father, I long for Your peace in my heart. Please take every
anxious thread, every tightly pulled knot of uncertainty, sorrow,
conflict, and disappointment into Your gentle, loving hands. Amen.*

Hold them in the highest regard in love because of
their work. Live in peace with each other.
1 THESSALONIANS 5:13 NIV

Therefore I exhort first of all that supplications, prayers,
intercessions, and giving of thanks be made for all men,
for kings and all who are in authority, that we may lead a
quiet and peaceable life in all godliness and reverence.
1 TIMOTHY 2:1–2 NKJV

Behold, how good and how pleasant it is for
brethren to dwell together in unity!
PSALM 133:1 KJV

Work at living in peace with everyone, and work at living a holy
life, for those who are not holy will not see the Lord.
HEBREWS 12:14 NLT

For, "THE ONE WHO DESIRES LIFE, TO LOVE AND SEE GOOD DAYS, MUST KEEP
HIS TONGUE FROM EVIL AND HIS LIPS FROM SPEAKING DECEIT. HE MUST TURN
AWAY FROM EVIL AND DO GOOD; HE MUST SEEK PEACE AND PURSUE IT."
1 PETER 3:10–11 NASB

Lord, no matter what happens to upset us on the surface,
You are in our innermost being, bringing peace and comfort.
Thank You that we can always trust You. Amen.

You will keep in perfect peace those whose minds
are steadfast, because they trust in you.
ISAIAH 26:3 NIV

For God has not given us a spirit of fear,
but of power and of love and of a sound mind.
2 TIMOTHY 1:7 NKJV

"I am leaving you with a gift—peace of mind and heart. And the peace
I give is a gift the world cannot give. So don't be troubled or afraid."
JOHN 14:27 NLT

When the presence of the Lord really becomes your experience,
you will actually discover that you have gradually begun to love
this silence and peaceful rest which come with His presence.
MADAME GUYON

Perseverance

You've tried everything to no avail. Now what? You've prayed for a loved one for years, but nothing changes. What do you do?

The Lord tells us that after we've done everything we know to do, and have said everything we know to say, to stand. In other words, persevere. Keep believing, praying, and standing in faith.

The same holds true for every area of our lives. We must hold steady in the face of adversity, doubt, or apparent failure. Why? Because God is faithful if we will only stand fast and persevere against all odds.

Thank You for Your promise to preserve me if I love You, Father. I know that this is an eternal promise. What more incentive do I need to pursue a right walk with You? Keep me on the right path, Lord. Amen.

For the which cause I also suffer these things: nevertheless I am not ashamed: for I know whom I have believed, and am persuaded that he is able to keep that which I have committed unto him against that day. Hold fast the form of sound words, which thou hast heard of me, in faith and love which is in Christ Jesus.

2 TIMOTHY 1:12–13 KJV

"He who has an ear, let him hear what the Spirit says to the churches. He who overcomes will not be hurt by the second death."

REVELATION 2:11 NASB

We have come to share in Christ, if indeed we
hold our conviction firmly to the very end.

HEBREWS 3:14 NIV

"To him who overcomes I will grant to sit with Me on My throne, as I also overcame and sat down with My Father on His throne."

REVELATION 3:21 NKJV

These trials will show that your faith is genuine. It is being tested as fire tests and purifies gold—though your faith is far more precious than mere gold. So when your faith remains strong through many trials, it will bring you much praise and glory and honor on the day when Jesus Christ is revealed to the whole world.

1 PETER 1:7 NLT

This burden is heavy, Lord. There are days when I don't know how much longer I can go on. But Your Word says that You will provide a way of escape. You help us carry our burdens. Thank You for Your promise. Amen.

Thou therefore endure hardness,
as a good soldier of Jesus Christ.
2 TIMOTHY 2:3 KJV

Though he fall, he shall not be utterly cast down;
for the LORD upholds him with His hand.
PSALM 37:24 NKJV

Let us hold tightly without wavering to the hope we affirm,
for God can be trusted to keep his promise.
HEBREWS 10:23 NLT

For I am persuaded, that neither death, nor life, nor angels,
nor principalities, nor powers, nor things present, nor things to
come, nor height, nor depth, nor any other creature, shall be able to
separate us from the love of God, which is in Christ Jesus our Lord.
ROMANS 8:38–39 KJV

It was for freedom that Christ set us free; therefore keep
standing firm and do not be subject again to a yoke of slavery.
GALATIANS 5:1 NASB

I want to be a fruitful vine, Lord. With Your help I can, whether the
fruit I bring is a cheerful attitude or money to help provide for
my family. Show me the best way to contribute to the
happiness of my home and family. Amen.

The path of the righteous is like the morning sun,
shining ever brighter till the full light of day.
PROVERBS 4:18 NIV

Then Jesus said to those Jews who believed Him,
"If you abide in My word, you are My disciples indeed."
JOHN 8:31 NKJV

You already know these things, dear friends. So be on guard;
then you will not be carried away by the errors of these
wicked people and lose your own secure footing.
2 PETER 3:17 NLT

Who shall separate us from the love of Christ?
Shall trouble or hardship or persecution or famine
or nakedness or danger or sword?
ROMANS 8:35 NIV

Therefore take up the whole armor of God, that you may be able
to withstand in the evil day, and having done all, to stand.
EPHESIANS 6:13 NKJV

Therefore, my brethren dearly beloved and longed for, my joy
and crown, so stand fast in the Lord, my dearly beloved.
PHILIPPIANS 4:1 KJV

*Thank You, Lord, for being so faithful. Thank You for Your
compassion—that is just the right amount to get
me through the day. Amen.*

Therefore, since we are surrounded by such a huge crowd of
witnesses to the life of faith, let us strip off every weight that slows
us down, especially the sin that so easily trips us up. And let us
run with endurance the race God has set before us. We do this by
keeping our eyes on Jesus, the champion who initiates and perfects
our faith. Because of the joy awaiting him, he endured the
cross, disregarding its shame. Now he is seated in
the place of honor beside God's throne.
HEBREWS 12:1–2 NLT

You may have to fight a battle more than once to win it.
MARGARET THATCHER

Power

*W*orkshops, conferences, books, and magazines all herald the attributes of empowerment and what it can mean in a woman's life. We long to fortify ourselves with the knowledge, wisdom, capabilities, and tools that will give us the power to become or do something greater than ourselves.

The scriptures talk a lot about power too—the power of God. As the Lord empowers us through the Holy Spirit, we change in ways we never dreamed and accomplish the seemingly impossible with His help. The truth is, self-empowerment often fades into futility, but God's power empowers the powerless continually.

Father, it often seems that might makes right and I stand no chance,
but I know Your power can overcome whatever evil men might plan.
When I am in despair, fill me with faith in Your justice. Amen.

Seek the LORD and His strength; seek His face continually.
1 CHRONICLES 16:11 NASB

"The LORD your God is with you, the Mighty Warrior who saves.
He will take great delight in you; in his love he will no longer
rebuke you, but will rejoice over you with singing."
ZEPHANIAH 3:17 NIV

Now to Him who is able to do exceedingly abundantly above all
that we ask or think, according to the power that works in us.
EPHESIANS 3:20 NKJV

For the Kingdom of God is not just a lot of talk;
it is living by God's power.
1 CORINTHIANS 4:20 NLT

*The stone still stood there in that quiet garden,
a reminder of the reality of the problem we all must live
with; but Christ had moved it to one side so very easily,
demonstrating His resurrection power on our behalf.*
JILL BRISCOE

Prayer

A mother prays for her child at the foot of a tear-stained bed. An elderly woman sits in a wheelchair interceding for her church. A grandmother kneels at the kitchen sink to pray for her grandchildren. A young woman sits in a classroom, whispering a prayer for a friend, and a little girl places her hand on her sick puppy and prays.

Prayer is simply talking to God. Lofty words and pious phrases are unnecessary—only a pure, honest, and sincere heart matters. God's power is unleashed through prayer. So pray often, anywhere, anytime.

Lord, when I see how You have interceded on my behalf, I want to fall on my face before You. My prayers have been answered in miraculous ways. In times when all I could see was darkness, You provided light and power and hope. Amen.

"At that time you won't need to ask me for anything. I tell you the truth, you will ask the Father directly, and he will grant your request because you use my name. You haven't done this before. Ask, using my name, and you will receive, and you will have abundant joy."

JOHN 16:23–24 NLT

But thou, when thou prayest, enter into thy closet, and when thou hast shut thy door, pray to thy Father which is in secret; and thy Father which seeth in secret shall reward thee openly. But when ye pray, use not vain repetitions, as the heathen do: for they think that they shall be heard for their much speaking.

MATTHEW 6:6–7 KJV

Give ear to my words, O LORD, consider my groaning. Heed the sound of my cry for help, my King and my God, for to You I pray.

PSALM 5:1–2 NASB

"And will give our attention to prayer and the ministry of the word."

ACTS 6:4 NIV

"If you then, being evil, know how to give good gifts to your children, how much more will your Father who is in heaven give good things to those who ask Him!"

MATTHEW 7:11 NKJV

Lord, I'm grateful that I can show my children where to turn in times of trouble. They don't have to try to do it all themselves, because we are all Your children. Amen.

Rejoice in our confident hope.
Be patient in trouble, and keep on praying.
Romans 12:12 nlt

Pray continually.
1 Thessalonians 5:17 niv

"You will make your prayer to Him, He will hear
you, and you will pay your vows."
Job 22:27 nkjv

Pray in the Spirit at all times and on every occasion. Stay alert
and be persistent in your prayers for all believers everywhere.
Ephesians 6:18 nlt

I waited patiently for the Lord; and he inclined
unto me, and heard my cry.
Psalm 40:1 kjv

"Now, will not God bring about justice for His elect who cry
to Him day and night, and will He delay long over them?"
Luke 18:7 nasb

"You can pray for anything, and if you
have faith, you will receive it."
Matthew 21:22 nlt

*Father, I get discouraged when I don't know which way to go.
Remind me that You are right behind me, telling me which way
to turn. Help me to be quiet and listen for Your guidance. Amen.*

"If my people, who are called by my name, will humble themselves and pray and seek my face and turn from their wicked ways, then I will hear from heaven, and I will forgive their sin and will heal their land."
2 CHRONICLES 7:14 NIV

Then you will call upon Me and go and pray to Me, and I will listen to you. And you will seek Me and find Me, when you search for Me with all your heart.
JEREMIAH 29:12–13 NKJV

The LORD is nigh unto all them that call upon him, to all that call upon him in truth.
PSALM 145:18 KJV

Let us therefore come boldly unto the throne of grace, that we may obtain mercy, and find grace to help in time of need.
HEBREWS 4:16 KJV

The sacrifice of the wicked is an abomination to the LORD, but the prayer of the upright is His delight.
PROVERBS 15:8 NASB

"It shall come to pass that before they call, I will answer; and while they are still speaking, I will hear."
ISAIAH 65:24 NKJV

"Ask and it will be given to you; seek and you will find; knock and the door will be opened to you. For everyone who asks receives; the one who seeks finds; and to the one who knocks, the door will be opened."
MATTHEW 7:7–8 NIV

Lord, one of the greatest gifts You've given me is the Holy Spirit to intercede for me during prayer. Thank You, Holy Spirit, for intervening and making my requests better than I ever could. Amen.

Confess your sins to each other and pray for each other so that you may be healed. The earnest prayer of a righteous person has great power and produces wonderful results.
JAMES 5:16 NLT

"Again I say to you, that if two of you agree on earth about anything that they may ask, it shall be done for them by My Father who is in heaven. For where two or three have gathered together in My name, I am there in their midst."
MATTHEW 18:19–20 NASB

Oh, that men would give thanks to the LORD for His goodness, and for His wonderful works to the children of men!
PSALM 107:15 NKJV

Well then, what shall I do? I will pray in the spirit, and I will also pray in words I understand. I will sing in the spirit, and I will also sing in words I understand.
1 CORINTHIANS 14:15 NLT

Yet the LORD will command his lovingkindness in the day time, and in the night his song shall be with me, and my prayer unto the God of my life.
PSALM 42:8 KJV

Therefore I want the men everywhere to pray lifting
up holy hands without anger or disputing.
1 Timothy 2:8 NIV

*Lord, I know not all prayers are answered, but many are,
so I continue to petition You, for You are my hope. Amen.*

"They caused the cry of the poor to come before him,
so that he heard the cry of the needy."
Job 34:28 NIV

*Lord, this language I speak is so inadequate to tell You what I want
to say. I can't begin to find the words to thank You for the
successes I have in my life. You are awesome. Amen.*

"He shall call upon Me, and I will answer him; I will be
with him in trouble; I will deliver him and honor him."
Psalm 91:15 NKJV

Because he bends down to listen, I will pray
as long as I have breath!
Psalm 116:2 NLT

Be anxious for nothing, but in everything by prayer and
supplication with thanksgiving let your requests be made known
to God. And the peace of God, which surpasses all comprehension,
will guard your hearts and your minds in Christ Jesus.
Philippians 4:6–7 NASB

Prayer is an indispensable part of our relationship with Jesus Christ.
Laurel Oke Logan

Pride

*H*ave you noticed that boasting has become an admirable attribute? (To clarify: Confidence in one's abilities or talents is different from bragging about them.) With much bravado, women from the boardroom to the catwalk herald their gifts and talents with more intensity than an on-the-scene journalist broadcasting breaking news.

Pride is not only admissible in the world, it's expected. To God, however, pride is sin. A proud and haughty spirit is unattractive and unacceptable to the King of kings. Besides, any king's daughter would rather brag about her heavenly Father's attributes than about her own.

Father, please don't let me fall into the trap of false pride. Whatever small beauty I bring into this world is only a tiny reflection of Your beauty, Your creation, Your perfection. Amen.

Do not be wise in your own eyes;
fear the LORD and shun evil.
PROVERBS 3:7 NIV

And He sat down, called the twelve, and said to them, "If anyone
desires to be first, he shall be last of all and servant of all."
MARK 9:35 NKJV

"But it is wrong to say God doesn't listen,
to say the Almighty isn't concerned."
JOB 35:13 NLT

A high look, and a proud heart,
and the plowing of the wicked, is sin.
PROVERBS 21:4 KJV

But as it is, you boast in your arrogance;
all such boasting is evil.
JAMES 4:16 NASB

*Lord, I'm called to live a godly life—not by childishness but by
Your grace and virtue. Thank You for Your provision. Amen.*

Live in harmony with one another. Do not be proud, but be willing
to associate with people of low position. Do not be conceited.
ROMANS 12:16 NIV

"Talk no more so very proudly; let no arrogance come from
your mouth, for the LORD is the God of knowledge;
and by Him actions are weighed."
1 SAMUEL 2:3 NKJV

As the Scriptures say, "If you want to boast, boast only about the
LORD." When people commend themselves, it doesn't count for
much. The important thing is for the Lord to commend them.
2 CORINTHIANS 10:17–18 NLT

How can ye believe, which receive honour one of another,
and seek not the honour that cometh from God only?
JOHN 5:44 KJV

*Lord, I need an attitude adjustment that can only come from
You. Let me be a cheerful worker. Resolve my conflicted
feelings and give me Your peace. Amen.*

All who fear the LORD will hate evil. Therefore, I hate pride
and arrogance, corruption and perverse speech.
PROVERBS 8:13 NLT

Pride goes before destruction,
and a haughty spirit before stumbling.
PROVERBS 16:18 NASB

For if a man think himself to be something,
when he is nothing, he deceiveth himself.
GALATIANS 6:3 KJV

For by the grace given me I say to every one of you: Do not think
of yourself more highly than you ought, but rather think
of yourself with sober judgment, in accordance with
the faith God has distributed to each of you.
ROMANS 12:3 NIV

*Why are we not far more frightened of what pride can do?
Pride can cost us—and probably those after us.*
BETH MOORE

Protection

*A*s women, we walk with caution to our car or on the street at night. We warn our daughters to guard themselves against possible intruders or attacks. Mothers use child-safety products to protect toddlers from harm, and we teach our children to avoid strangers and to look both ways before crossing the street.

Similarly, God protects us. He provides a refuge in life's storms with the assurance that He is with us in every situation. He takes extra precaution to guide, assist, instruct, and protect us each day. He is our help, our shield, and our best protection.

Lord, I thank You for Your guidance and protection day after day. Although I never know what the day will bring, You have a plan and I trust in You. Amen.

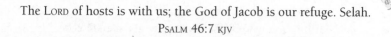

The LORD of hosts is with us; the God of Jacob is our refuge. Selah.
PSALM 46:7 KJV

In the fear of the LORD there is strong confidence,
and his children will have refuge.
PROVERBS 14:26 NASB

"When you pass through the waters, I will be with you; and when
you pass through the rivers, they will not sweep over you.
When you walk through the fire, you will not be
burned; the flames will not set you ablaze."
ISAIAH 43:2 NIV

But the LORD has been my defense,
and my God the rock of my refuge.
PSALM 94:22 NKJV

Be my rock of safety where I can always hide. Give the order
to save me, for you are my rock and my fortress.
PSALM 71:3 NLT

*Father, as long as I trust in Your presence, I have nothing to worry
about. Nothing can separate me from You, because You are the strong
protector, the mighty One who watches over me always.
I praise You, Lord, for Your protection. Amen.*

Above all, taking the shield of faith, wherewith ye shall
be able to quench all the fiery darts of the wicked.
EPHESIANS 6:16 KJV

For it is You who blesses the righteous man, O Lord,
You surround him with favor as with a shield.
PSALM 5:12 NASB

The name of the Lord is a strong fortress;
the godly run to him and are safe.
PROVERBS 18:10 NLT

Our soul waiteth for the Lord: he is our help and our shield.
PSALM 33:20 KJV

Every word of God is tested; He is a shield
to those who take refuge in Him.
PROVERBS 30:5 NASB

*There are times, Lord, when I feel as if You've forgotten me.
How could I let those feelings of being forsaken overwhelm me?
Help me to remember that the Creator of the entire
universe holds me in His hands! Amen.*

He will cover you with his feathers, and under his wings you will
find refuge; his faithfulness will be your shield and rampart.
PSALM 91:4 NIV

"But whoever listens to me will dwell safely,
and will be secure, without fear of evil."
PROVERBS 1:33 NKJV

He sang: "The LORD is my rock, my fortress, and my savior; my God is my rock, in whom I find protection. He is my shield, the power that saves me, and my place of safety. He is my refuge, my savior, the one who saves me from violence. I called on the LORD, who is worthy of praise, and he saved me from my enemies."
2 SAMUEL 22:2–4 NLT

For You are my rock and my fortress; therefore,
for Your name's sake, lead me and guide me.
PSALM 31:3 NKJV

The LORD is my rock, my fortress and my deliverer;
my God is my rock, in whom I take refuge, my shield
and the horn of my salvation, my stronghold.
PSALM 18:2 NIV

Lord, Your promise of protection gives me a secure feeling.
I'm surrounded by Your love and protection. Because You love
me and care for me, I can do the same for my children.
Thank You for the peace this brings. Amen.

The LORD is good, a strong hold in the day of trouble;
and he knoweth them that trust in him.
NAHUM 1:7 KJV

181

Cast your burden upon the LORD and He will sustain you;
He will never allow the righteous to be shaken.
PSALM 55:22 NASB

God is our refuge and strength, always ready to help in times
of trouble. So we will not fear when earthquakes come and the
mountains crumble into the sea. Let the oceans roar and
foam. Let the mountains tremble as the waters surge!
PSALM 46:1–3 NLT

The eternal God is thy refuge,
and underneath are the everlasting arms.
DEUTERONOMY 33:27 KJV

The LORD also will be a stronghold for the oppressed,
a stronghold in times of trouble.
PSALM 9:9 NASB

God is our refuge and strength,
an ever-present help in trouble.
PSALM 46:1 NIV

*God will never lead you where
His strength cannot keep you.*
BARBARA JOHNSON

Purity

Christians take heart. Purity is gaining popularity. Teenagers across the country are vowing abstinence by wearing "purity rings." The silver band symbolizes a teen's vow to celibacy until marriage—it is an expression of his or her love and commitment to God and the promise to live a pure life.

Whether we are fourteen or fifty, the pledge to purity can begin anytime and carry throughout our lifetime. God calls every believer to a life of holiness without fornication, adultery, or impurity. A pure life is a fully consecrated one, with or without a symbolic ring.

Lord, I want to help bring others to You, to be judged a virtuous woman for Your sake, not for any glory that might come to me. Use me as You see fit, because any work You give me is an honor. Amen.

Drink water from your own cistern,
and running water from your own well.
PROVERBS 5:15 NKJV

So put to death the sinful, earthly things lurking within you.
Have nothing to do with sexual immorality, impurity, lust,
and evil desires. Don't be greedy, for a greedy person is an
idolater, worshiping the things of this world. Because of
these sins, the anger of God is coming.
COLOSSIANS 3:5–6 NLT

But fornication, and all uncleanness, or covetousness, let it
not be once named among you, as becometh saints.
EPHESIANS 5:3 KJV

"You shall not commit adultery."
EXODUS 20:14 NASB

*A person of purity stands before his peers and superiors
and courageously maintains his faith in God.*
CINDY TRENT

Repentance

*W*hat is repentance? To regret you bought those expensive shoes? To wish you hadn't opened your mouth, or to kick yourself for not speaking up?

To *repent* means to change one's mind, yes. But it also means to turn *away* from sin and turn *toward* God. The Lord cannot forgive us of our sins until we repent of them and turn to Him for salvation.

Did you know that there is a good kind of sorrow? It's the sorrow that leads us to repentance (2 Corinthians 7:10). As we repent, God forgives and our new life begins.

Thank You, Jesus, for calling sinners to repentance. If You had come only for the righteous, I would not have been called, for I am a sinner. I thank You for Your mercy. Amen.

For the sorrow that is according to the will of God produces
a repentance without regret, leading to salvation, but the
sorrow of the world produces death.
2 Corinthians 7:10 NASB

The Lord is not slack concerning His promise, as some count
slackness, but is longsuffering toward us, not willing that any
should perish but that all should come to repentance.
2 Peter 3:9 NKJV

"God overlooked people's ignorance about these things in
earlier times, but now he commands everyone everywhere
to repent of their sins and turn to him."
Acts 17:30 NLT

I will have mercy, and not sacrifice: for I am not come to
call the righteous, but sinners to repentance.
Matthew 9:13 KJV

"In the same way, I tell you, there is joy in the presence
of the angels of God over one sinner who repents."
Luke 15:10 NASB

*There is no condemnation for us when we believe in You, Jesus.
The covering of Your blood helps us to prevail over anything.
We never need to fear anymore. Thank You for
giving us this victory. Amen.*

"Remember, therefore, what you have received and heard; hold it fast, and repent. But if you do not wake up, I will come like a thief, and you will not know at what time I will come to you."
REVELATION 3:3 NIV

Or do you despise the riches of His goodness, forbearance, and longsuffering, not knowing that the goodness of God leads you to repentance?
ROMANS 2:4 NKJV

"He will sing to men and say, 'I have sinned and perverted what is right, and it is not proper for me. He has redeemed my soul from going to the pit, and my life shall see the light.'"
JOB 33:27–28 NASB

Rend your heart and not your garments. Return to the LORD your God, for he is gracious and compassionate, slow to anger and abounding in love, and he relents from sending calamity.
JOEL 2:13 NIV

"Now repent of your sins and turn to God, so that your sins may be wiped away."
ACTS 3:19 NLT

Given unto You Lord, You told me to give and that if
I do, it shall be given to me. You don't say what "it" is,
but Your generosity is unmatched and Your blessings
are always wonderful. Thank You! Amen.

The LORD is nigh unto them that are of a broken heart;
and saveth such as be of a contrite spirit.
PSALM 34:18 KJV

"Therefore repent of this wickedness of yours, and pray the Lord
that, if possible, the intention of your heart may be forgiven you."
ACTS 8:22 NASB

Come near to God and he will come near to you. Wash your hands,
you sinners, and purify your hearts, you double-minded.
JAMES 4:8 NIV

We long for revival, but revival begins with repentance.
NATALIE GRANT

Rest

$\mathcal{M}$ost women are doers, proficient in multitasking. We cook dinner as we do laundry and assist our kids with homework. We schedule appointments via cell phone while we grocery shop. We answer emails while paying bills. And the moment we stop, our minds spin as we relive the day.

Although rest is essential to our spiritual, physical, and emotional health, it often gets lost like a stray sock in the dryer. God wants His people to rest, and this section of scriptures emphasizes the benefits of, and need for, a break.

So take a breather. Rest.

Heavenly Father, I find it hard to find time to relax. Thank You for making me to lie down even when I don't want to. Thank You for leading me beside quiet waters when I need the solace. Amen.

I will both lay me down in peace, and sleep: for thou,
LORD, only makest me dwell in safety.
PSALM 4:8 KJV

For He has said somewhere concerning the seventh day:
"AND GOD RESTED ON THE SEVENTH DAY FROM ALL HIS WORKS". . .
So there remains a Sabbath rest for the people of God.
HEBREWS 4:4, 9 NASB

"And you would be secure, because there is hope; yes,
you would dig around you, and take your rest in safety."
JOB 11:18 NKJV

Those who live in the shelter of the Most High will
find rest in the shadow of the Almighty.
PSALM 91:1 NLT

Rest in the LORD, and wait patiently for him: fret not thyself
because of him who prospereth in his way, because of
the man who bringeth wicked devices to pass.
PSALM 37:7 KJV

*Again and again, I've found Him faithful to respond, and the
closer I move to Him, the safer I feel and the better I rest.*
PATSY CLAIRMONT

Righteousness

What is righteousness? What can we do to attain it? Is right living the ticket? Or is there something more we should know or do?

The definition of *righteousness* includes the following: "a quality or character of uprightness; an attribute of God and whatever or whoever conforms to the revealed will of God."

Contrary to what some believe, God's righteousness is only attainable through faith in Christ, not through obedience to a prescribed set of laws or good deeds (Ephesians 2:8–9).

Do you desire righteousness? Accept Christ and follow His Word.

Do you not know that the unrighteous will not inherit the kingdom of God?

Father, on my worst days I feel totally unworthy. But I know You have promised to cleanse me from all unrighteousness, to wipe away my guilt and make me whole if I confess my sins. Amen.

Do not be deceived. Neither fornicators, nor idolaters,
nor adulterers, nor homosexuals, nor sodomites.
1 CORINTHIANS 6:9 NKJV

"Seek the Kingdom of God above all else, and live righteously,
and he will give you everything you need."
MATTHEW 6:33 NLT

Lord, who shall abide in thy tabernacle? who shall dwell in
thy holy hill? He that walketh uprightly, and worketh
righteousness, and speaketh the truth in his heart.
PSALM 15:1–2 KJV

"He does not withdraw His eyes from the righteous; but with kings
on the throne He has seated them forever, and they are exalted."
JOB 36:7 NASB

*Lord, You stand before the throne of Your Father and claim me as
Your own, exempt from sin and judgment. Because of Your
sacrifice, I am made worthy. Thank You. Amen.*

All your words are true; all your righteous laws are eternal.
PSALM 119:160 NIV

"Then the righteous will shine forth as the sun in the kingdom
of their Father. He who has ears to hear, let him hear!"
MATTHEW 13:43 NKJV

"But if you truly obey his voice and do all that I say, then I will be
an enemy to your enemies and an adversary to your adversaries."
EXODUS 23:22 NASB

The LORD hears his people when they call to him for help.
He rescues them from all their troubles.
PSALM 34:17 NLT

Whereby are given unto us exceeding great and precious promises:
that by these ye might be partakers of the divine nature, having
escaped the corruption that is in the world through lust.
2 PETER 1:4 KJV

*Lord, You are made strong in my weaknesses. I need Your help to
remember that I should count it all joy when I am
faced with trials and suffering. Amen.*

You who love the LORD, hate evil! He preserves the souls of His
saints; He delivers them out of the hand of the wicked. Light is
sown for the righteous, and gladness for the upright in heart.
PSALM 97:10–11 NKJV

The eyes of the LORD are upon the righteous,
and his ears are open unto their cry.
PSALM 34:15 KJV

"If you fully obey the LORD your God and carefully keep all his
commands that I am giving you today, the LORD your God
will set you high above all the nations of the world."
DEUTERONOMY 28:1 NLT

The LORD will not allow the righteous to hunger,
but He will reject the craving of the wicked.
PROVERBS 10:3 NASB

If we confess our sins, he is faithful and just and will forgive
us our sins and purify us from all unrighteousness.
1 John 1:9 niv

Whoever pursues righteousness and unfailing love
will find life, righteousness, and honor.
Proverbs 21:21 nlt

But know that the Lord hath set apart him that is godly
for himself: the Lord will hear when I call unto him.
Psalm 4:3 kjv

"Then He will answer them, 'Truly I say to you, to the extent
that you did not do it to one of the least of these, you did not
do it to Me.' These will go away into eternal punishment,
but the righteous into eternal life."
Matthew 25:45–46 nasb

The righteous will rejoice in the Lord and take refuge
in him; all the upright in heart will glory in him!
Psalm 64:10 niv

For He made Him who knew no sin to be sin for us,
that we might become the righteousness of God in Him.
2 Corinthians 5:21 nkjv

We do not have to be qualified to be holy.
Madeleine L' Engle

Salvation

*I*n the world, work is a prerequisite to achievement. In God's Word, works are meaningless without faith in Christ. Salvation is God's free gift to anyone who confesses her sins and asks Jesus into her heart and life. Why? Because Jesus paid the price for our sins when He died on the cross—and by accepting Him, we are given salvation and eternal life.

Have you asked Jesus into your heart? If not, He stands at your door and knocks. All you need do is invite Him in. Go ahead. He's been waiting awhile.

Lord, guide me so that all I am and do will point the way for others, that they also can enjoy the benefits of salvation and join their voices in praise of Your Father in heaven. Amen.

This means that anyone who belongs to Christ is a new person.
The old life is gone; a new life has begun!
2 CORINTHIANS 5:17 NLT

My little children, these things write I unto you, that ye sin
not. And if any man sin, we have an advocate with the Father,
Jesus Christ the righteous: and he is the propitiation for our sins:
and not for ours only, but also for the sins of the whole world.
1 JOHN 2:1–2 KJV

This is good and acceptable in the sight of God our Savior,
who desires all men to be saved and to come to
the knowledge of the truth.
1 TIMOTHY 2:3–4 NASB

Yet to all who did receive him, to those who believed in his name,
he gave the right to become children of God—children born
not of natural descent, nor of human decision or
a husband's will, but born of God.
JOHN 1:12–13 NIV

"He who believes in the Son has everlasting life;
and he who does not believe the Son shall not see
life, but the wrath of God abides on him."
JOHN 3:36 NKJV

*Heavenly Father, my greatest responsibility as Your child is to share
the gift of salvation with others. My family, my neighbors,
my coworkers—so many people need to hear Your Word.
Make me attentive to each opportunity You present to me. Amen.*

"There is salvation in no one else! God has given no other name
under heaven by which we must be saved."
ACTS 4:12 NLT

But after that the kindness and love of God our Saviour toward
man appeared, not by works of righteousness which we have
done, but according to his mercy he saved us, by the washing
of regeneration, and renewing of the Holy Ghost; which he
shed on us abundantly through Jesus Christ our Saviour.
TITUS 3:4–6 KJV

Just as I also please all men in all things, not seeking my own
profit but the profit of the many, so that they may be saved.
1 CORINTHIANS 10:33 NASB

Jesus replied, "Very truly I tell you, no one can see the kingdom
of God unless they are born again." "How can someone be born
when they are old?" Nicodemus asked. "Surely they cannot enter a
second time into their mother's womb to be born!" Jesus answered,
"Very truly I tell you, no one can enter the kingdom of God unless
they are born of water and the Spirit. Flesh gives birth to flesh,
but the Spirit gives birth to spirit. You should not be
surprised at my saying, 'You must be born again.' "
JOHN 3:3–7 NIV

*Christ has made all things right. I had nothing to
do but accept it as a free gift from Him.*
HANNAH WHITALL SMITH

Scripture

*I*s the Bible just an ancient history book? What significance do the scriptures have in modern society?

As the following verses indicate, the scriptures are the life-giving, soul-sustaining, power-packed, anointed words of God! They provide us with the spiritual nutrients necessary for daily living.

God's Word reveals God's will and character to us, bringing salvation, healing, deliverance, hope, peace, wisdom, guidance, and restoration to those who read its pages.

Just an ancient history book inapplicable to today's lifestyle and issues? Read on.

Father, I know it is Your will for me to understand Your Word, and You've given me the Holy Spirit to guide me. Help me to take advantage of this great blessing. Amen.

Let the word of Christ dwell in you richly in all wisdom, teaching and admonishing one another in psalms and hymns and spiritual songs, singing with grace in your hearts to the Lord.
COLOSSIANS 3:16 NKJV

I have hidden your word in my heart,
that I might not sin against you.
PSALM 119:11 NLT

And that from a child thou hast known the holy scriptures, which are able to make thee wise unto salvation through faith which is in Christ Jesus.
2 TIMOTHY 3:15 KJV

Your word is a lamp to my feet and a light to my path.
PSALM 119:105 NASB

Fix these words of mine in your hearts and minds; tie them as symbols on your hands and bind them on your foreheads. Teach them to your children, talking about them when you sit at home and when you walk along the road, when you lie down and when you get up.
DEUTERONOMY 11:18–19 NIV

Lord, as I read and study Your Word and hear sermons preached about it, I still have questions and much to learn. I ask that You give me a clear understanding of what You are saying to me through it. Amen.

For the word of God is living and powerful, and sharper than
any two-edged sword, piercing even to the division of soul
and spirit, and of joints and marrow, and is a discerner
of the thoughts and intents of the heart.

HEBREWS 4:12 NKJV

God, after He spoke long ago to the fathers in the prophets in many
portions and in many ways, in these last days has spoken to us
in His Son, whom He appointed heir of all things,
through whom also He made the world.

HEBREWS 1:1–2 NASB

"This Book of the Law shall not depart from your mouth, but you
shall meditate in it day and night, that you may observe to do
according to all that is written in it. For then you will make
your way prosperous, and then you will have good success."

JOSHUA 1:8 NKJV

Searching what, or what manner of time, the Spirit of Christ who
was in them was indicating when He testified beforehand the
sufferings of Christ and the glories that would follow. To them it
was revealed that, not to themselves, but to us they were ministering
the things which now have been reported to you through those
who have preached the gospel to you by the Holy Spirit sent
from heaven—things which angels desire to look into.

1 PETER 1:11–12 NKJV

*How much of a calm and gentle spirit you achieve, then, will depend
on how regularly and consistently, persistently and obediently
you partake of the Word of God, your spiritual food.*

SHIRLEY RICE

Seeking God

I once lost my then-small son in an interactive playroom at Disney World. Panic set in as I scoured every area. About to notify security, I raced to the escalator where Jeff stood sobbing. "Where were you?" he whimpered, as if I were the one who was lost.

Similarly, God isn't lost—we are. Our search for Him begins when we realize that. Most of us seek God when we're afraid, discouraged, sick, or sad. But God desires for us to seek Him because we yearn to know Him. These passages reveal how God blesses and rewards those who diligently seek Him.

Father, my daily problems come and go; yet if I remain steadfast and dedicated, doing the work You have given me to do, I am confident that my reward awaits me. Thank You, Lord. Amen.

But seek ye first the kingdom of God, and his righteousness;
and all these things shall be added unto you.
MATTHEW 6:33 KJV

Sow with a view to righteousness, reap in accordance with
kindness; break up your fallow ground, for it is time to seek
the LORD until He comes to rain righteousness on you.
HOSEA 10:12 NASB

Look to the LORD and his strength; seek his face always.
1 CHRONICLES 16:11 NIV

Glory in His holy name; let the hearts of
those rejoice who seek the LORD!
1 CHRONICLES 16:10 NKJV

"If you look for me wholeheartedly, you will find me."
JEREMIAH 29:13 NLT

*Lord, there are many times when I need You and Your Word to
guide me. Lead me and help me become an overcomer. Amen.*

Seek the LORD, and ye shall live.
AMOS 5:6 KJV

One thing have I desired of the LORD, that will I seek after;
that I may dwell in the house of the LORD all the days of my life,
to behold the beauty of the LORD, and to enquire in his temple.
PSALM 27:4 KJV

At night my soul longs for You, indeed, my spirit within me seeks
You diligently; for when the earth experiences Your judgments
the inhabitants of the world learn righteousness.
ISAIAH 26:9 NASB

"But from there you will search again for the LORD your God.
And if you search for him with all your heart
and soul, you will find him."
DEUTERONOMY 4:29 NLT

Therefore if you have been raised up with Christ, keep seeking the
things above, where Christ is, seated at the right hand of God.
COLOSSIANS 3:1 NASB

*Help me invest my time in more worthy pursuits, Lord, ones that
will provide lasting satisfaction. I'm not sure what You will ask
of me, but I am willing to try anything You recommend
and give any resulting praise to You. Amen.*

Glory in his holy name; let the hearts
of those who seek the LORD rejoice.
1 CHRONICLES 16:10 NIV

"Then if my people who are called by my name will humble
themselves and pray and seek my face and turn from their
wicked ways, I will hear from heaven and will forgive
their sins and restore their land."
2 CHRONICLES 7:14 NLT

The young lions lack and suffer hunger; but those
who seek the LORD shall not lack any good thing.
PSALM 34:10 NKJV

*For it is impossible to be in the presence
of Jesus and not be changed.*
JOANNA WEAVER

Self-Control

*P*astries line the table. "Have one," the hostess says. "Thanks, but I'm dieting," you respond. "One won't hurt," she prods, handing you a chocolate tart. Soon one tart turns into three with a side of strawberry cheesecake. "I'll resume my diet tomorrow," you reason, self-control scrambling away faster than rats from a burning building.

When we act, say, go, or do what we shouldn't, we lose control—and end up regretting it. The Bible teaches that self-control and moderation is achievable. Our desires may tempt us, but they don't have to control us. Even while we're dieting!

Father, Your Holy Spirit is telling me that self-control is not one of my strengths and I need to work on it. I need temperance. Help me turn things over to You and allow You to develop self-control in my life. Amen.

Then Pilate said to Him, "Do You not hear how many things they testify against You?" And He did not answer him with regard to even a single charge, so the governor was quite amazed.
MATTHEW 27:13–14 NASB

But even the archangel Michael, when he was disputing with the devil about the body of Moses, did not himself dare to condemn him for slander but said, "The Lord rebuke you!"
JUDE 9 NIV

For to this you were called, because Christ also suffered for us, leaving us an example, that you should follow His steps: "Who committed no sin, nor was deceit found in His mouth"; who, when He was reviled, did not revile in return; when He suffered, He did not threaten, but committed Himself to Him who judges righteously.
1 PETER 2:21–23 NKJV

Do you like honey? Don't eat too much, or it will make you sick!
PROVERBS 25:16 NLT

Charity suffereth long, and is kind; charity envieth not; charity vaunteth not itself, is not puffed up, doth not behave itself unseemly, seeketh not her own, is not easily provoked, thinketh no evil.
1 CORINTHIANS 13:4–5 KJV

Lord, keep me on the right path when my own plans are flawed, because only You know where You need me to be today and tomorrow. Amen.

Let your gentle spirit be known to all men. The Lord is near.
PHILIPPIANS 4:5 NASB

Older men are to be temperate, dignified, sensible,
sound in faith, in love, in perseverance.
TITUS 2:2 NASB

Because we belong to the day, we must live decent lives for all
to see. Don't participate in the darkness of wild parties and
drunkenness, or in sexual promiscuity and immoral living,
or in quarreling and jealousy. Instead, clothe yourself with
the presence of the Lord Jesus Christ. And don't let yourself
think about ways to indulge your evil desires.
ROMANS 13:13–14 NLT

And beside this, giving all diligence, add to your faith virtue;
and to virtue knowledge; and to knowledge temperance;
and to temperance patience; and to patience godliness.
2 PETER 1:5–6 KJV

Everyone who competes in the games goes into strict training.
They do it to get a crown that will not last, but we
do it to get a crown that will last forever.
1 CORINTHIANS 9:25 NIV

*Father, help me show others my need for self-control, to not give
in to the temptation of sin. Only when we turn from sin can
we truly gain understanding in all wisdom. We ask for
Your strength to help in this. Amen.*

Let him sit alone and keep silent, because God has laid it on him;
let him put his mouth in the dust—there may yet be hope.
LAMENTATIONS 3:28–29 NKJV

For if you live according to the flesh you will die; but if by the
Spirit you put to death the deeds of the body, you will live.
ROMANS 8:13 NKJV

And we are instructed to turn from godless living and sinful
pleasures. We should live in this evil world with wisdom,
righteousness, and devotion to God.
TITUS 2:12 NLT

Or do you not know that wrongdoers will not inherit the kingdom
of God? Do not be deceived: Neither the sexually immoral nor
idolaters nor adulterers nor men who have sex with men nor thieves
nor the greedy nor drunkards nor slanderers nor swindlers will
inherit the kingdom of God. And that is what some of you were.
But you were washed, you were sanctified, you were justified in
the name of the Lord Jesus Christ and by the Spirit of our God.
1 CORINTHIANS 6:9–11 NIV

Rules for proper behavior keep us from getting hurt.
We risk our own life and the lives of others when we
give in to our desires, whatever they might be.
LINDA BARTLETT

Sin

$\mathcal{S}$ ome think that sin is too harsh a word. So they use euphemisms for sin such as mistake, blunder, fault, offense, or violation, which sound much better. We might try to whitewash it, but sin is just that—sin.

The scriptures define *sin* as knowing to do good but not doing it. No one is blameless. We have all sinned and are in need of repentance and forgiveness.

Jesus came to fix the sin problem. Just ask Him. He's not afraid of the word *sin*—He conquered it!

Father, every day is a battle. I struggle between following You and choosing what feels right at the moment. I need Your wisdom and power to persevere toward a true change of heart and action. But, most of all, I need Your forgiveness. Amen.

But if we walk in the Light as He Himself is in the Light,
we have fellowship with one another, and the blood
of Jesus His Son cleanses us from all sin.
1 JOHN 1:7 NASB

"Come now, let us settle the matter," says the LORD. "Though your
sins are like scarlet, they shall be as white as snow; though they
are red as crimson, they shall be like wool."
ISAIAH 1:18 NIV

"For this is My blood of the new covenant,
which is shed for many for the remission of sins."
MATTHEW 26:28 NKJV

But he was pierced for our rebellion, crushed for our sins. He was
beaten so we could be whole. He was whipped so we could be
healed. All of us, like sheep, have strayed away. We have left God's
paths to follow our own. Yet the LORD laid on him the sins of us all.
ISAIAH 53:5–6 NLT

My little children, these things write I unto you, that ye sin
not. And if any man sin, we have an advocate with the Father,
Jesus Christ the righteous: And he is the propitiation for our sins:
and not for ours only, but also for the sins of the whole world.
1 JOHN 2:1–2 KJV

*Lord, help me study Your Word and grow in knowledge
of You in order to attain godliness. Then I can be an
example to others of how to live a godly life. Amen.*

"Of Him all the prophets bear witness that through His name
everyone who believes in Him receives forgiveness of sins."
Acts 10:43 NASB

Here is a trustworthy saying that deserves full acceptance:
Christ Jesus came into the world to save
sinners—of whom I am the worst.
1 Timothy 1:15 NIV

Who Himself bore our sins in His own body on the tree, that we,
having died to sins, might live for righteousness—
by whose stripes you were healed.
1 Peter 2:24 NKJV

He has removed our sins as far from us as the east is from the west.
Psalm 103:12 NLT

Knowing this, that our old man is crucified with him, that the
body of sin might be destroyed, that henceforth we should
not serve sin. For he that is dead is freed from sin.
Romans 6:6–7 KJV

Who gave Himself for our sins so that He might rescue us from this
present evil age, according to the will of our God and Father.
Galatians 1:4 NASB

It is the very nature of sin to prevent man
from meditating on spiritual things.
Mary Martha Sherwood

211

Sincerity

*S*incerity is as welcoming as nestling in a cozy chair in front of a fire on a brisk, cold day.

The motives behind what we say or do are at the core of a sincere heart. Are our motives pure and genuine? Or do we possess a selfish, hidden agenda? Someone who demonstrates sincerity of heart and pure motives is a person whom we can trust.

Similarly, God expects us to approach Him in a straightforward manner with unadulterated sincerity. Hypocrisy has no place in our relationship with Him. God knows our heart and He seeks one seeped in sincerity.

Father, I know that I tend to get focused on the negatives,
and sometimes my thoughts are crowded with impatience,
envy, anger, or resentment. Please help me focus on You.
Fill me with pure thoughts. Amen.

Blessed is the one whose sin the LORD does not count
against them and in whose spirit is no deceit.
PSALM 32:2 NIV

And in their mouth was found no deceit, for they are
without fault before the throne of God.
REVELATION 14:5 NKJV

So prepare your minds for action and exercise self-control.
Put all your hope in the gracious salvation that will come
to you when Jesus Christ is revealed to the world.
1 PETER 1:13 NLT

But let us, who are of the day, be sober, putting on the breastplate
of faith and love; and for an helmet, the hope of salvation.
1 THESSALONIANS 5:8 KJV

Like newborn babies, long for the pure milk of the word,
so that by it you may grow in respect to salvation.
1 PETER 2:2 NASB

*Lord, I'm ashamed to admit that sometimes I have a hard time taking
You at Your Word. Please show me how to trust You more, even when
my mind can't grasp it and my heart can't accept it. Amen.*

Grace to all who love our Lord Jesus
Christ with an undying love.
EPHESIANS 6:24 NIV

For we are not, as so many, peddling the word of God; but as of sincerity, but as from God, we speak in the sight of God in Christ.
2 CORINTHIANS 2:17 NKJV

"So fear the LORD and serve him wholeheartedly. Put away forever the idols your ancestors worshiped when they lived beyond the Euphrates River and in Egypt. Serve the LORD alone."
JOSHUA 24:14 NLT

Now that you have purified yourselves by obeying the truth so that you have sincere love for each other, love one another deeply, from the heart.
1 PETER 1:22 NIV

What will you do in the appointed day, and in the day of the feast of the LORD?
HOSEA 9:5 NKJV

Father, I know You blessed me abundantly in the family You have given me. Help me not to flaunt them or to take the credit that belongs to You. Amen.

We can say with confidence and a clear conscience that we have
lived with a God-given holiness and sincerity in all our dealings.
We have depended on God's grace, not on our own human
wisdom. That is how we have conducted ourselves
before the world, and especially toward you.
2 CORINTHIANS 1:12 NLT

Therefore, rid yourselves of all malice and all deceit,
hypocrisy, envy, and slander of every kind.
1 PETER 2:1 NIV

For our exhortation was not of deceit, nor of uncleanness,
nor in guile: but as we were allowed of God to be put in trust
with the gospel, even so we speak; not as pleasing men, but God,
which trieth our hearts. For neither at any time used we flattering
words, as ye know, nor a cloke of covetousness; God is witness.
1 THESSALONIANS 2:3–5 KJV

Therefore let us celebrate the feast, not with old leaven,
nor with the leaven of malice and wickedness, but with
the unleavened bread of sincerity and truth.
1 CORINTHIANS 5:8 NASB

For I say, through the grace given to me, to everyone who is among you, not to think of himself more highly than he ought to think, but to think soberly, as God has dealt to each one a measure of faith.
ROMANS 12:3 NKJV

Lord, I ask for Your help in raising my children. May Your patience and kindness be made visible through my actions. Amen.

For I want you to understand what really matters, so that you may live pure and blameless lives until the day of Christ's return.
PHILIPPIANS 1:10 NLT

I speak not by commandment, but by occasion of the forwardness of others, and to prove the sincerity of your love.
2 CORINTHIANS 8:8 KJV

Speaking beautifully is little to the purpose
unless one lives beautifully.
ELIZABETH PRENTISS

Sobriety

Sobriety includes several areas of behavior. Some scriptures refer to soberness as soundness of mind or exhibiting self-control. In other verses, sobriety addresses the negative influence of alcohol and intoxicants.

Either way, these passages direct us to be filled with God's Spirit rather than substances or attitudes that will control and destroy our lives. The damages intoxicants inflict are far-reaching, leading us into bondage. The scriptures warn us to flee from the things that have the potential to harm ourselves and others. So be sober, filled to overflowing with the Holy Spirit.

I've made mistakes, Lord. But someday You will present me faultless,
cleansed by Your blood. The evidence of Your power to lift me
up and make me whole fills me with exceeding joy.
I praise You forever and forever. Amen.

"For he will be great in the sight of the Lord. He is never to take wine or other fermented drink, and he will be filled with the Holy Spirit even before he is born."
LUKE 1:15 NIV

Wine produces mockers; alcohol leads to brawls. Those led astray by drink cannot be wise.
PROVERBS 20:1 NLT

Woe unto them that rise up early in the morning, that they may follow strong drink; that continue until night, till wine inflame them!
ISAIAH 5:11 KJV

"They have also cast lots for My people, traded a boy for a harlot and sold a girl for wine that they may drink."
JOEL 3:3 NASB

Who has woe? Who has sorrow? Who has strife? Who has complaints? Who has needless bruises? Who has bloodshot eyes? Those who linger over wine, who go to sample bowls of mixed wine. Do not gaze at wine when it is red, when it sparkles in the cup, when it goes down smoothly! In the end it bites like a snake and poisons like a viper.
PROVERBS 23:29–32 NIV

Lord, help me to rely only on You when times are difficult. May I not depend on anything else to ease my burdens. Amen.

"Now therefore, please be careful not to drink wine or
similar drink, and not to eat anything unclean."
JUDGES 13:4 NKJV

"What sorrow awaits you who make your neighbors drunk!
You force your cup on them so you can gloat over
their shameful nakedness."
HABAKKUK 2:15 NLT

And take heed to yourselves, lest at any time your hearts
be overcharged with surfeiting, and drunkenness, and cares
of this life, and so that day come upon you unawares.
LUKE 21:34 KJV

Like tangled thorns, and like those who are drunken with their
drink, they are consumed as stubble completely withered.
NAHUM 1:10 NASB

For drunkards and gluttons become poor,
and drowsiness clothes them in rags.
PROVERBS 23:21 NIV

"Abstain," says God. He doesn't say, "Be careful" or "Pray about it."
He says, "Abstain! Run from it! Don't touch it! Have nothing to do with
it!" Stay pure and blameless. If you don't, God will suffer most of all.
ANNE ORTLUND

Strength

*W*hy do we wait until our strength is depleted before we seek God? Women carry the weight of the world on their shoulders. We worry about our families as we manage our homes and assist our friends, churches, and communities. We maintain busy schedules as we transport kids to soccer practice and school functions. We cook, clean, work, and care for aging parents. No wonder we run out of steam!

Yet God wants us to rely upon His strength, not ours—to exchange our weakness for His power. What are you waiting for? Seek God's strength.

Father God, though Your strength is limitless, it's tempered with wisdom and gentleness. You are both my strong tower and my tender, loving Father. Help me to find that proper balance of gentle strength in my own life. Amen.

"For the eyes of the LORD run to and fro throughout the whole earth, to show Himself strong on behalf of those whose heart is loyal to Him. In this you have done foolishly; therefore from now on you shall have wars."

2 CHRONICLES 16:9 NKJV

"Wealth and honor come from you alone, for you rule over everything. Power and might are in your hand, and at your discretion people are made great and given strength."

1 CHRONICLES 29:12 NLT

Finally, my brethren, be strong in the Lord,
and in the power of his might.

EPHESIANS 6:10 KJV

In purity, in knowledge, in patience, in kindness, in the Holy Spirit, in genuine love, in the word of truth, in the power of God; by the weapons of righteousness for the right hand and the left.

2 CORINTHIANS 6:6–7 NASB

He gives strength to the weary and increases the power of the weak.

ISAIAH 40:29 NIV

Make my heart perfect, Lord. Take my hand, and give me strength. Be strong for me when I don't measure up. My way to attain a perfect heart is through You, Lord, so don't take Your eyes off me. Amen.

Wait on the LORD; be of good courage, and He shall strengthen your heart; wait, I say, on the LORD!

PSALM 27:14 NKJV

221

The LORD gives his people strength.
The LORD blesses them with peace.
PSALM 29:11 NLT

Because of Your strength, Lord, I can smile. When I need peace,
You strengthen me on the inside. This is where I need You
the most. Let me reflect Your strength so that my
children will be drawn to You also. Amen.

"The righteous keep moving forward, and those with
clean hands become stronger and stronger."
JOB 17:9 NLT

That ye might walk worthy of the Lord unto all pleasing, being
fruitful in every good work, and increasing in the knowledge of
God; strengthened with all might, according to his glorious
power, unto all patience and longsuffering with joyfulness.
COLOSSIANS 1:10–11 KJV

O God, You are awesome from Your sanctuary. The God of Israel
Himself gives strength and power to the people. Blessed be God!
PSALM 68:35 NASB

But he said to me, "My grace is sufficient for you, for my power
is made perfect in weakness." Therefore I will boast all the more
gladly about my weaknesses, so that Christ's power may rest on me.
2 CORINTHIANS 12:9 NIV

We must continue to ask God for wisdom and insight and for
the strength to persevere. He will cause us to rise up
and fly like eagles, walking and not fainting.
NORMA SMALLEY

Temptation

*J*esus fasted and prayed in the wilderness for forty days, and the devil tempted Him, albeit unsuccessfully.

Our Savior faced temptation, and so do we. Although it presents itself in different forms, temptation is what Satan uses to defeat, discourage, and pollute the believer's mind and heart. He will use every nasty trick and deceptive device to get us to sin.

But don't worry. Martin Luther once said that we can't stop a bird from flying over our heads, but we can prevent it from building a nest there. Temptation will come—but it need not set up housekeeping.

Lord, I am human and often tempted. Be with me when I am tempted and show me the true joys of self-control. Amen.

Let no man say when he is tempted, I am tempted of God: for God cannot be tempted with evil, neither tempteth he any man.

JAMES 1:13 KJV

"And do not lead us into temptation, but deliver us from evil. [For Yours is the kingdom and the power and the glory forever. Amen."]

MATTHEW 6:13 NASB

If this is so, then the Lord knows how to rescue the godly from trials and to hold the unrighteous for punishment on the day of judgment.

2 PETER 2:9 NIV

"Watch and pray, lest you enter into temptation. The spirit indeed is willing, but the flesh is weak."

MATTHEW 26:41 NKJV

There hath no temptation taken you but such as is common to man: but God is faithful, who will not suffer you to be tempted above that ye are able; but will with the temptation also make a way to escape, that ye may be able to bear it.

1 CORINTHIANS 10:13 KJV

Temptations come, as a general rule, when they are sought.

MARGARET OLIPHANT

Truth

Your child gets in trouble at school. You question her, insisting on the whole truth. The doctor has bad news. You want the truth, despite your fear and hesitation.

In situations like these, truth becomes all-important. Yet truth is even more essential in our walk with God.

In the Bible, the idea of *truth* carries four interpretations: 1) actual, true to fact; 2) real, ideal, genuine; 3) dealing faithfully or truly with others; and 4) truth in all its fullness and scope, as embodied in Jesus, showing sincerity and integrity of character. To know Jesus is to know the truth.

Lord, let me know when I am wrong. That way I can come to You for cleansing and an opportunity to make things right. Thank You for the truth in Your Word, even though sometimes the truth hurts. Amen.

Buy the truth, and do not sell it,
also wisdom and instruction and understanding.
PROVERBS 23:23 NKJV

For the LORD is good. His unfailing love continues forever,
and his faithfulness continues to each generation.
PSALM 100:5 NLT

Jesus saith unto him, I am the way, the truth, and the life:
no man cometh unto the Father, but by me.
JOHN 14:6 KJV

"The Rock! His work is perfect, for all His ways are just; a God of
faithfulness and without injustice, righteous and upright is He."
DEUTERONOMY 32:4 NASB

Finally, brothers and sisters, whatever is true, whatever is
noble, whatever is right, whatever is pure, whatever is lovely,
whatever is admirable—if anything is excellent or
praiseworthy—think about such things.
PHILIPPIANS 4:8 NIV

*I'm ashamed to admit that I often speak before I think, and the
words that come out of my mouth are not always truthful.
Please help me be a good example. Amen.*

"And you shall know the truth, and the truth shall make you free."
JOHN 8:32 NKJV

"All who invoke a blessing or take an oath will do so by
the God of truth. For I will put aside my anger
and forget the evil of earlier days."
ISAIAH 65:16 NLT

For the word of the LORD is right; and all his
works are done in truth.
PSALM 33:4 KJV

"For their sakes I sanctify Myself, that they
themselves also may be sanctified in truth."
JOHN 17:19 NASB

"These are the things you are to do: Speak the truth to each other,
and render true and sound judgment in your courts."
ZECHARIAH 8:16 NIV

For the law was given through Moses,
but grace and truth came through Jesus Christ.
JOHN 1:17 NKJV

*If we are Christians, we have committed ourselves to the
Lord Jesus Christ who said, "I am the Truth." In giving
ourselves to Him, we dedicate ourselves to the truth
not only about Him but about ourselves.*
PAMELA HOOVER HEIM

Understanding

$\mathcal{E}$leanor Roosevelt said, "Understanding is a two-way street." We'd all like to be understood, but do we understand? To gain understanding we must consider another's perspective apart from our own. In essence, we must walk in their shoes.

Knowing God gives us a greater appreciation for and understanding of others. As we view people and life through His eyes, our viewpoint changes. The things we once questioned, we now perceive with greater clarity and purpose.

To understand rather than to be understood is every Christian woman's quest for spiritual maturity. To understand while seldom understood is that quest realized.

Lord, help me to be understanding with everyone I come into contact with, to encourage rather than discourage. I want to take their hands and walk with them, as You've taken time to walk with me. Amen.

Joyful is the person who finds wisdom, the one who gains understanding. For wisdom is more profitable than silver, and her wages are better than gold. Wisdom is more precious than rubies; nothing you desire can compare with her.
PROVERBS 3:13–15 NLT

Then shalt thou understand the fear of the LORD, and find the knowledge of God. For the LORD giveth wisdom: out of his mouth cometh knowledge and understanding.
PROVERBS 2:5–6 KJV

They will not hurt or destroy in all My holy mountain, for the earth will be full of the knowledge of the LORD as the waters cover the sea. Then in that day the nations will resort to the root of Jesse, who will stand as a signal for the peoples; and His resting place will be glorious.
ISAIAH 11:9–10 NASB

For wisdom will enter your heart, and knowledge will be pleasant to your soul. Discretion will protect you, and understanding will guard you. Wisdom will save you from the ways of wicked men, from men whose words are perverse.
PROVERBS 2:10–12 NIV

Therefore if there is any consolation in Christ, if any comfort of love, if any fellowship of the Spirit, if any affection and mercy, fulfill my joy by being like-minded, having the same love, being of one accord, of one mind.
PHILIPPIANS 2:1–2 NKJV

*Lord, I know so many parents who don't try to see things through others'
eyes and who are not sympathetic to the trials they face. I don't
want to be like that. Help me to be like You, Lord. Amen.*

When I was a child, I used to speak like a child, think like
a child, reason like a child; when I became a man,
I did away with childish things.
1 CORINTHIANS 13:11 NASB

Wisdom is found on the lips of the discerning,
but a rod is for the back of one who has no sense.
PROVERBS 10:13 NIV

But You, O Lord, are a God full of compassion, and gracious,
longsuffering and abundant in mercy and truth.
PSALM 86:15 NKJV

"And this is what he says to all humanity: 'The fear of the
Lord is true wisdom; to forsake evil is real understanding.'"
JOB 28:28 NLT

With the ancient is wisdom; and in length of days
understanding. With him is wisdom and strength,
he hath counsel and understanding.
JOB 12:12–13 KJV

*Lord, I'm grateful that I have the opportunity to teach my children
the truths that are found in Your Word. I'm trusting that You will
open their spiritual understanding. I am looking forward to
the day that they will accept You as Savior. Amen.*

Wisdom rests in the heart of one who has understanding,
but in the hearts of fools it is made known.
PROVERBS 14:33 NASB

"But let the one who boasts boast about this: that they have the
understanding to know me, that I am the LORD, who exercises
kindness, justice and righteousness on earth, for in
these I delight," declares the LORD.
JEREMIAH 9:24 NIV

Foolishness brings joy to those with no sense;
a sensible person stays on the right path.
PROVERBS 15:21 NLT

The mind of the prudent acquires knowledge,
and the ear of the wise seeks knowledge.
PROVERBS 18:15 NASB

For if you possess these qualities in increasing measure,
they will keep you from being ineffective and unproductive
in your knowledge of our Lord Jesus Christ.
2 PETER 1:8 NIV

Father, I know my understanding is weak. But when I am in need of guidance, the first place I turn to is Your Word. Help me to search diligently, for I know the answers I need are there. Amen.

Make me understand the way of Your precepts;
so shall I meditate on Your wonderful works.
PSALM 119:27 NKJV

Rich people may think they are wise, but a poor person
with discernment can see right through them.
PROVERBS 28:11 NLT

Teach me good judgment and knowledge:
for I have believed thy commandments.
PSALM 119:66 KJV

Yearn to understand first and to be understood second.
BECA LEWIS ALLEN

Wisdom

*A*ccording to Webster's dictionary, *wisdom* is "the power of judging correctly, following the soundest course of action based on knowledge, experience, understanding and good judgment."

God is wisdom personified. His wisdom far exceeds our most impressive reaches of thought. The scriptures explain that "the foolishness of God is wiser than men; and the weakness of God is stronger than men" (1 Corinthians 1:25 KJV). God alone is the source of true wisdom. Accordingly, we should seek His wisdom and discernment in every decision we make. To do so is just plain wise.

Lord, I need Your gentle wisdom for every area of life.
I'm so thankful that what You offer is the best. Amen.

Be wise now therefore, O ye kings:
be instructed, ye judges of the earth.
PSALM 2:10 KJV

Those who obey him will not be punished. Those who are
wise will find a time and a way to do what is right.
ECCLESIASTES 8:5 NLT

Say to wisdom, "You are my sister," and call
understanding your intimate friend.
PROVERBS 7:4 NASB

Therefore do not be foolish, but understand what the Lord's will is.
EPHESIANS 5:17 NIV

"Therefore whoever hears these sayings of Mine, and does them,
I will liken him to a wise man who built his house on the rock: and
the rain descended, the floods came, and the winds blew and beat
on that house; and it did not fall, for it was founded on the rock."
MATTHEW 7:24–25 NKJV

*Lord, please give me the strength and the wisdom to be the godly
example that my children need to see. I know that the life
I live will have a profound influence on the attitudes
my children develop concerning You. Amen.*

It is foolish to belittle one's neighbor; a sensible person keeps quiet.
PROVERBS 11:12 NLT

A prudent man foreseeth the evil, and hideth himself:
but the simple pass on, and are punished.
PROVERBS 22:3 KJV

A prudent man conceals knowledge,
but the heart of fools proclaims foolishness.
PROVERBS 12:23 NKJV

Good comes to those who lend money generously
and conduct their business fairly.
PSALM 112:5 NLT

He that handleth a matter wisely shall find good: and whoso
trusteth in the LORD, happy is he. The wise in heart shall be called
prudent: and the sweetness of the lips increaseth learning.
PROVERBS 16:20–21 KJV

*Lord, show me how to establish wisdom and give me the
strength to stand firm in those convictions. Amen.*

Whoever is wise, let him understand these things; whoever is
discerning, let him know them. For the ways of the LORD
are right, and the righteous will walk in them,
but transgressors will stumble in them.
HOSEA 14:9 NASB

My son, pay attention to what I say; turn your ear to my words.
Do not let them out of your sight, keep them within your heart; for
they are life to those who find them and health to one's whole body.
PROVERBS 4:20–22 NIV

The law of the wise is a fountain of life, to turn one away from
the snares of death. Good understanding gains favor,
but the way of the unfaithful is hard.
PROVERBS 13:14–15 NKJV

235

How much better it is to get wisdom than gold!
And to get understanding is to be chosen above silver.
PROVERBS 16:16 NASB

"To him belong strength and insight; both deceived and deceiver are
his. He leads rulers away stripped and makes fools of judges."
JOB 12:16–17 NIV

*Father, please give me the wisdom I need to properly advise my
children. Help me teach them to seek guidance from Your
Word and in communion with the Holy Spirit. Amen.*

My son, eat honey because it is good, and the honeycomb which
is sweet to your taste; so shall the knowledge of wisdom be
to your soul; if you have found it, there is a prospect,
and your hope will not be cut off.
PROVERBS 24:13–14 NKJV

In that day he will be your sure foundation, providing a rich
store of salvation, wisdom, and knowledge. The fear
of the LORD will be your treasure.
ISAIAH 33:6 NLT

I will instruct thee and teach thee in the way which
thou shalt go: I will guide thee with mine eye.
PSALM 32:8 KJV

But if any of you lacks wisdom, let him ask of God, who gives to all
generously and without reproach, and it will be given to him.
JAMES 1:5 NASB

The simple believe anything, but the prudent
give thought to their steps.
PROVERBS 14:15 NIV

*Lord, help me realize that my understanding is not necessary for
the completion of Your plan. You understand everything;
all I need to do is have faith. Amen.*

For wisdom is protection just as money is protection,
but the advantage of knowledge is that wisdom
preserves the lives of its possessors.
ECCLESIASTES 7:12 NASB

However, we speak wisdom among those who are mature, yet not
the wisdom of this age, nor of the rulers of this age, who are
coming to nothing. But we speak the wisdom of God in a mystery,
the hidden wisdom which God ordained before the ages for our
glory, which none of the rulers of this age knew; for had they
known, they would not have crucified the Lord of glory.
1 CORINTHIANS 2:6–8 NKJV

And if any man think that he knoweth any thing,
he knoweth nothing yet as he ought to know.
1 CORINTHIANS 8:2 KJV

*Learning is not attained by chance, it must be sought
for with ardor and attended to with diligence.*
ABIGAIL ADAMS

Zeal

*W*hat comes to mind when you hear the word *zeal*? Slobbering sports fans? Wild-eyed fanatics? For most of us, those images aren't terribly appealing.

But the Bible's picture of zeal is different. It's an image of commitment—of God to His people, and His people back to Him. Scriptural zeal is a beautiful thing, a strong desire to do right by God and His creation.

You can't go wrong being zealous for God. A passion for serving Him—by serving the people around you—doesn't make you a fanatic. It makes you like Jesus!

Father, help me to be diligent in understanding You and Your precepts.
Please give me a continuous desire to know You better. Amen.

For zeal for your house consumes me, and the
insults of those who insult you fall on me.
PSALM 69:9 NIV

Whatsoever thy hand findeth to do, do it with thy might;
for there is no work, nor device, nor knowledge,
nor wisdom, in the grave, whither thou goest.
ECCLESIASTES 9:10 KJV

He put on righteousness like a breastplate, and a helmet of
salvation on His head; and He put on garments of vengeance
for clothing and wrapped Himself with zeal as a mantle.
ISAIAH 59:17 NASB

Even so you, since you are zealous for spiritual gifts, let it be
for the edification of the church that you seek to excel.
1 CORINTHIANS 14:12 NKJV

As many as I love, I rebuke and chasten:
be zealous therefore, and repent.
REVELATION 3:19 KJV

Zeal will do more than knowledge.
WILLIAM HAZLITT